MARCO ⊕ POLO

Travel with
**Insider
Tips**

TENERIFE

ATLANTIC
OCEAN

Azores (Port.)

Madeira (Port.)

Canary Islands
(Spain)

Tenerife

Western
Sahara

The best Insider Tips → p. 4

INSIDER TIP

Best of ... → p. 6

The Northwest → p. 32

The Northeast → p. 52

SYMBOLS

INSIDER TIP   Insider Tip
★   Highlight
●●●●   Best of ...
☼   Scenic view

☺ Responsible travel: fair
  trade principles and the
  environment respected

(*) Telephone numbers that
    are not toll-free

PRICE CATEGORIES HOTELS

Expensive	over 150 euros
Moderate	70–150 euros
Budget	under 70 euros

Prices for a double room per
night, with breakfast (in a hotel); without breakfast (in an
apartment)

PRICE CATEGORIES RESTAURANTS

Expensive	over 20 euros
Moderate	10–20 euros
Budget	under 10 euros

Prices for a meal with starter
and main course (no drinks)

On the cover: La Laguna – Tenerife's cultural centre p. 54 | A trip into the laurel forest p. 96

CONTENTS

The National Park → p. 68

The Southeast → p. 72

The Southwest → p. 78

Road atlas → p. 126

MAPS IN THE GUIDEBOOK
(128 A1) Page numbers and
coordinates refer to the road
atlas
(0) Site/address located off
the map. Coordinates are
also given for places that are
not marked on the road atlas

Maps for Puerto de la Cruz
and Santa Cruz de Tenerife
can be found inside the back
cover

**INSIDE BACK COVER:
PULL-OUT MAP →**

Map for Playa de las Améri-
cas/Los Cristianos → p. 86

PULL-OUT MAP 𝕄
(𝕄 A1) Refers to the remova-
ble pull out map

The best MARCO POLO Insider Tips

Our top 15 Insider Tips

INSIDER TIP **Festival fervour**

The largest pilgrimage on the Canary Islands attracts tens of thousands of devotees. To celebrate Candlemas, the faithful descend on Candelaria – some even by boat → **p. 111**

INSIDER TIP **Living in style**

The former mansion in La Quinta Roja in Garachico has been transformed into a delightful country hotel – with patio, roof terrace, good food and wine → **p. 35**

INSIDER TIP **The great outdoors**

Away from the coast Tenerife can offer plenty of breathtaking encounters with nature. Dedicated active holidaymakers choose to stay in the Luz del Mar in Los Silos → **p. 38**

INSIDER TIP **Pleasures for the palate**

Predominantly vegetarian – the food in the El Calabacín is superfresh. The chef is much admired for his imaginative cuisine → **p. 47**

INSIDER TIP **Fish, fresh off the boat**

Las Aguas and San Andrés, two coastal villages in the northeast, are popular places for islanders at weekends. The sea breeze must whet their appetite, because the restaurants do a roaring trade serving (usually) fresh fish and seafood → **p. 65**

INSIDER TIP **Good food and inexpensive**

La Hierbita or 'Little Herb' in Tenerife's capital city is very popular with young people. There is a wide selection of tapas, generous portions of Canarian fare, plus plenty of local wines → **p. 63**

INSIDER TIP **Among shepherds and farmers**

Located in the cloud-covered laurel forest is a small visitor centre that provides information on walks in the Montañas de Anaga. Lower down there is an ancient track, recently upgraded into a sensory trail. It only takes an hour, but that's long enough to appreciate the full beauty of the 'enchanted forest' → **p. 59**

BEST OF ...

FOR FREE

● *A park above the town*
From the coastal vantage point in *Puerto de la Cruz* climb up winding trails past waterfalls and on to the *Parque Taoro* (photo). At the top stand and admire the grand, old-style hotel and the verdant lawns fringed by subtropical plants → p. 46

● *A natural swimming pool*
Ignore the waves crashing against the sea wall sending plumes of spray high into the air, while you swim serenely in the *natural pools of Bajamar*. Few other places in the north offer the same safe bathing opportunities → p. 53

● *From fruit market to art showroom*
The *Centro de Arte La Recova* used to be a busy fruit market hall in Santa Cruz, but now it is used to display art – photographs, avant-garde and the out-of-the-ordinary → p. 66

● *Fine winery*
Do make a detour to this large farmstead in El Sauzal with its fine traditional architecture and panoramic sea views. The building houses the *Casa del Vino*, a winery selling Tenerife's best vintages, plus you can follow the story of wine production on the island → p. 27, 67

● *Visitor centre in the National Park*
In the *Centro de Visitantes El Portillo* you can be part of the island's geological history. The volcanic tunnel quakes, red-hot lava flows and the room rumbles. Round off your visit with a tour of the botanical rock garden replete with native alpine flora → p. 71

● *A picture-book landscape*
'... I have never beheld a prospect more varied, more attractive, more harmonious in the distribution of the masses of verdure and rocks than the western coast of Tenerife,' wrote Alexander von Humboldt in 1799, when he first saw the Valle de la Orotava. A lookout point with stunning views (plus café) has been built in his memory → p. 32

●●●● Dots in guidebook refer to 'Best of ...' tips

● *A dragon tree with no dragons*
It has become one of Tenerife's trademarks. Although the tree with its lush crown is actually a type of lily, it can live for up to 1,000 years. The largest drago grows in Icod de los Vinos → p. 38

● *A Canarian delicacy*
It's a cereal, roasted and finely ground – *gofio,* the nutrient-rich staple food of the island's original inhabitants. Frowned upon for a long time as poor man's food, it is now a popular ingredient in the new Canarian cuisine, e.g. in *El Duende* → p. 24, 48

● *Gaze into space*
Stand on the roof of the island and pretend you're an actor in a science-fiction film – the metallic white towers of the *Observatorio del Teide* (photo) look straight up into the clear blue sky → p. 71

● *The pine tree – a survivor*
In the forest belt below the Cañadas grows the Canarian pine. With its extremely long needles it 'combs' moisture from the clouds, while the thick bark protects it from fire. One outstanding example is the *Pino Gordo* → p. 77

● *Sun-ripened*
Many of the exotic fruits that can grow in the 'eternal spring' are made into jams, chutneys and compotes. For the best selection visit *Delicias del Sol* in Chío – everything here is organic → p. 95

● *Stone pyramids*
In many parts of the island stones are carefully laid to create rural and urban walls. But in Güímar they were arranged in layers to create mysterious pyramids. These fascinating relics suggest that even before Christopher Columbus the Canary Islands were a staging post between the Old and the New World → p. 75

● *Filigree rosettes*
The women of Vilaflor have made a virtue out of necessity. To supplement the family budget, in the evening they get together and make lace rosettes. In this mountain village bed covers, table lace and shawls are still made using the traditional method → p. 77

ONLY IN

BEST OF ...

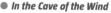

AND IF IT RAINS
Activities to brighten your day

● *In the Cave of the Wind*
High above Icod de los Vinos and running deep inside the flanks of Mount Teide is one of the world's longest lava tunnels. A short section of it is open to the public. But first of all do check out the displays inside the Cueva del Viento Visitor Centre, which explain how the tunnel came into being → p. 40

● *Lost in space*
The most interesting museum in La Laguna is the *Museo de la Ciencia*, which aims to unravel some of the mysteries of the cosmos. The Milky Way, supernovae, black holes – all are clearly explained → p. 55

● *Art Nouveau?*
A cleverly designed avant-garde building – the *TEA* (Tenerife Espacio de Arte, photo) stages temporary exhibitions to bring new art to the public's attention, but there is also a permanent exhibition of pieces by the surrealist, Tenerife-born artist, Óscar Domínguez → p. 62

● *In the shopping mall*
Stroll, browse and shop on seven floors for the latest fashions sorted by brand, cosmetics, perfume and jewellery. The food and drink section at *El Corte Inglés* is also impressive → p. 64

● *A pyramid with life inside*
Colonnades, temples and right in the middle the *Pirámide de Arona* – modelled on classical antiquity in downtown Playa de las Américas. There's a show every night in the pyramid. No gladiators, instead a troupe of flamenco dancers fired up by passion → p. 89

● *The bustle of the market hall*
At the weekend everyone makes a pilgrimage to the market (the one in *Adeje* is always lively). Fresh produce supplied by local farmers at affordable prices. Round off the morning with glass of wine and a tapa in the market bar → p. 90

RAIN

RELAX AND CHILL OUT
Take it easy and spoil yourself

● *Enjoy a sundowner in style*
If you love to watch the sun set, while sipping a cooling drink, then the beach bar at the Villa Cortés is the place to go. Order a beer and watch the windsurfers riding the waves for one last time → **p. 86**

● *A white aquatic landscape*
Lago de Martíanez in Puerto de la Cruz is a vast pool area designed with many curving contours (photo). Palm trees provide shade and palisade fences keep the city clamour away → **p. 106**

● *In the shadow of exotic plants*
In the *Jardín Botánico* in Puerto de la Cruz, tropical plants, some over 200 years old, form a primeval jungle. Sit by the pond or the fountain and let body and soul unwind → **p. 46**

● *Refuel in the Hotel Mencey*
After a stroll in the capital, Santa Cruz, you can regain your strength in the Mencey. This grand hotel in the old style has a club bar, a garden café and the restaurant is undoubtedly one of the best on the island → **p. 64**

● *Relax in Oriental style*
The island's newest spa is also the smartest one – it's in the south and occupies a majestic location overlooking a beautiful beach. As the name *Thai Zen SPAce* suggests, the treatments follow Oriental relaxation techniques → **p. 88**

● *Dreaming by the sea*
The beach at *Bahía del Duque* is small, but beautiful. The hours will fly by while you're spread out on a lounger beneath a bamboo parasol. Food and drink served in the ornate, blue and white pavilion → **p. 90**

● *Los Roques de García*
If you get up early or leave it until later on in the afternoon, you will have the spectacular view from the *Mirador de Los Roques* pretty well all to yourself → **p. 70**

INTRODUCTION

DISCOVER TENERIFE!

No, it's not lost any of its fascination. Planes circle it at respectful distance, before heading in to land. Visible from many miles, it shows the way. It's become a symbol for the island. Often dense cloud cover separates it from the world below. The Pico del Teide is the king of all volcanoes, surveying from his great height the hostile lunar landscape below. For us it's still an impressive sight, but for our forebears it was greatly feared. There was an eruption on its northern slopes as recently as 1909, but by then the island's geology was well understood.

No one 'discovered' the island, as it is visible from the African coast, but perhaps that explains why so many legends from antiquity have survived. Passing mariners couldn't fail to see the white tip and so for the Romans it was *Nivaria* or the 'snowy one'. The Guanches, Tenerife's first settlers, feared that an angry god, Guayote, was orchestrating Teide's eruptions. Columbus saw the sparks and smoke it spat out as a bad omen for his first voyage of discovery. In 1799 Alexander von Humboldt was struck by the fact that at daybreak the first rays of sunshine illuminated the summit,

Photo: La Orotava and Mount Teide

The north coast of the island is often wild, steep and rugged, as here near Las Aguas

while on the coast darkness still reigned. The Canarian day begins and ends on Mount Teide, at 3,718m (12,198ft) Spain's highest mountain. Despite the southern location of the Canary Islands, it often wears a snow cap in winter.

The inverted triangle covers an area of 2,034 sq km (785 sq miles) and it is the largest of the seven Islands of Eternal Spring, as the Canaries were known in the era of Homer. It is certainly large enough to reveal many contrasts: a blue ocean, great beaches, rugged cliffs, deep gorges, dense forests, barren wastes and Mount Teide volcano rising out of a bizarre sea of lava – all-in-all an opulent display of nature's diversity. Wander through colonial towns, explore museums and churches – culturally Tenerife has a lot to offer. Sit with the locals in down-to-earth bars, enjoy their traditional food, drink their strong wines and share in their lively festivals. Surf, dive,

Since 1100 BC
During their voyages of discovery the Phoenicians and later the Carthaginians arrive on the Canary Islands. First mention by Homer and Hesiod

5th century BC
Probably the first settlement on the archipelago by Berber tribes from North Africa

1496
The Spaniard Alonso Fernández de Lugo conquers Tenerife, the last of all the islands in the archipelago, and founds the settlement now called La Laguna

1701
Monks establish the first university on the Canary Islands in La Laguna

walk, cycle, turn night into day or simply lie back and relax – there is no place for boredom on Tenerife. And the sun will keep shining – throughout the whole year.

But many people get a shock when they arrive. The south is bleak and parched. It quickly becomes apparent that water is a rare and precious commodity here. Once great forests

Water is a rare and precious commodity

extended across Tenerife, streams trickled down from the mountains. But at the end of the 15th century the Spanish colonists set about exploiting both man and nature. First they subjugated the Guanches and then they felled the laurel and pine trees, on whose long needles the moisture from the clouds clung, before it dripped to the ground. Erosion followed, Tenerife's ecosystem had been badly damaged. Today, pine forests are only found in the interior, the laurel survives in the Anaga Mountains in the northeast.

Other native plants have been more successful. The Canarian palm, for example, with its thick trunk and spreading crown grows throughout the valleys, the *cardón*, the candelabra euphorbia, thrives in dry areas, as do the shrubby *tabaiba*, another euphorbia, and the *tajinaste*, a type of borage. In April at lower altitudes the viper's bugloss produces white umbels, higher up in the uplands from May to June the flowers take on a more reddish-violet hue. At higher altitudes you will see *retama*, a white-flowering variety of broom, and also *codeso*, the bright yellow cytisus. Cacti, almond trees, eucalyptus and all kinds of fruit trees arrived with the island's conquerors and have since put down strong roots everywhere in their new habitat. However, bananas, vines and all the colourful decorative flowers in public spaces in the resorts survive only as a result of constant irrigation.

The Guanches, and later the Europeans, preferred to settle in the cool upland plateau of La Laguna and in the Valle de la Orotava, Tenerife's green lung. They get the benefit of the northeast trade winds. Moist winds blow constantly against the north coast of Tenerife at altitudes of between 700–1,700m, but the central highlands block their passage. The clouds that form deposit rainfall and provide shade, which in turn lowers the temperature and helps to supply the vegetation with water. It's always cooler in these parts than in the south of the island. However, there is no need to fear the

1706
The volcanic eruption of Montaña Negra destroys large parts of the port of Garachico, but in the process new land forms in the northwest of Tenerife, now called Isla Baja

1797
Admiral Horatio Nelson invades Santa Cruz, but is repulsed

1852
Queen Isabel II grants the Canary Islands the status of a free trade zone, British influence grows thereafter

End of 19th Century
The cultivation and export of bananas brings economic prosperity to Tenerife

torrid heat of Africa – the dark continent is only some 300km (180 miles) away. The climate here is surprisingly benign. It is indeed like an eternal spring, which means mild temperatures – barely over 30° C in summer, rarely below 20° C. Warm trade winds and the cool Canarian current in the Atlantic help to maintain a steady balance. Several times a year, however, the island experiences the *calima,* a hot, dusty desert wind that blows directly across from the Sahara. It often hangs over the archipelago for several days. The air never seems to move and breathing can be difficult. When the wind moves away, a fine layer of desert sand remains on buildings and on plants.

The holiday areas have simply everything today's tourists could wish for

The holiday destinations of Los Cristianos and Playa de las Américas in the south have simply everything today's tourists could wish for. In just 50 years, an otherwise barren region has been transformed by beach resorts with apartment complexes, hotels and amusement parks – some call it a tourist ghetto. A hundred years ago, however, Puerto de la Cruz in the north was a retreat for well-heeled English visitors escaping miserable winters back home. Many took lodgings in the former port of La Orotava. Locals and visitors found the arrangement to be of mutual benefit. The tourists enjoyed a well-established urban setting and the Canary islanders were perfectly happy to do business with them.

But if you really want to get to know the country and the people, then you need to explore the island in greater depth. Almost one third of the 800,000 *tinerfeños* live in the *zona metropolitana,* as the old and the new capitals, La Laguna and Santa Cruz respectively, are known. A lot has happened here in recent years. The historic centre

1927
Tenerife, La Palma, La Gomera and Hierro combine to create the Province of Santa Cruz de Tenerife

1936
General Franco stages a military coup on Tenerife and forms a bridgehead for an assault on the government in Madrid

1960 onwards
The island enjoys steady growth with the advent of cheap air travel and package holidays

1986
Spain becomes a member of the European Union

2009–11
The global financial crisis hits Tenerife hard. Unemployment rises to over 25 percent

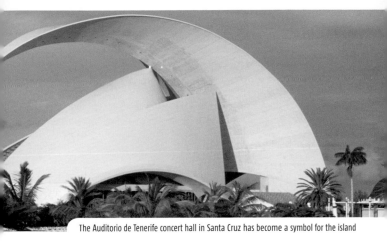

The Auditorio de Tenerife concert hall in Santa Cruz has become a symbol for the island

of La Laguna has been completely restored and it now enjoys Unesco World Heritage Site status. In Santa Cruz, internationally renowned architects were commissioned to design emblematic buildings, such as the Auditorium, the Congress Hall and the TEA Arts Centre. There were many ambitious plans for the future, e.g. a facelift for the sea front as far as the beach in San Andrés 10km (6 miles) away. But as a result of the global financial crisis all these grandiose plans have had to be shelved. Once the flow of cheap money came to halt in 2009, the construction sector, the driving force behind the Spanish economy, began to stutter. Tens of thousands of workers lost their jobs. Now no longer able to service their debts, many of them were forced to

> **In the countryside there's a world that harks back to a different era**

hand their homes back to the bank. But visitors will hardly notice the impact on everyday life. Despite the adverse circumstances, the Canary islanders stay cheerful. The general view is: 'We can't change anything, so what's the point of complaining?' And so the Canary islanders keep celebrating at carnival time, call in at the café or their favourite bar, take a late evening stroll and stop everything for a siesta between 1pm and 5pm.

If you explore the countryside, however, you will be surprised to find a world that harks back to a different era. You will see farmers loading up their donkeys, old men passing the time of day on the plaza and women dressed in black labouring in the fields. A rather spartan lifestyle continues very much as it did half a century ago all over Tenerife. At the beginning of the 20th century, thousands of *tinerfeños* emigrated to South America and to Cuba to escape famine at home. Today thankfully the word emigration belongs to the past. Despite all the crises of the present day, the Canary islanders are as one with the entire Spanish nation – they will overcome.

WHAT'S HOT

1 Be energy aware

Go green The festival of renewable energy takes place in the *Parque Eólic*. Powered solely by wind energy, this music event also promotes the benefits of other forms of green electricity *(www.eolica.es)*. Throughout the year, the *Instituto Tecnologico y de Energias Renovables* keeps consumers informed about the latest developments in green energy. There is even an educational trail, which illustrates the benefits of alternatives, such as photovoltaic solar panels, wind and geothermal energy *(Granadilla de Abona, www.iter.es, photo)*. And the trams are part of it too. Given the plentiful sunshine, it's no surprise arrays of PV panels are able to supply the tram network with all the power it needs *(www.tranviatenerife.com)*.

2

Tenerife Art

Island art There's a cheerful atmosphere at the time of the *MUECA* street art festival in Puerto de la Cruz *(www.festivalmueca.com, photo)*. No less cheerful are the abstract pieces by the German exile, *Karinia Loskarn (www.karinia-teneriffa.com)*. *Rosa Hernandez* is a visual artist, who finds inspiration in the island's natural forces *(www.rosahernandez.com)*.

3 La Laguna

New life La Laguna is back on the map again, especially in the former capital's tapas bars and bodegas *(www. aytolalaguna.com)*. It's now a fashionable spot for young islanders and there's a real buzz in the Old Town in the evening. The two bars, *Tasca El Tonique (Calle Sánchez Heraclio 23)* and *La Tasca Sacristía (Bencomo Calle 26)*, are popular meeting places, as is the *Posada de los Mosqueteros (Calle Santo Domingo, 24)*.

Get a good night's sleep

Sustainable accommodation You will sleep well and with a clear conscience in the *Casas Bioclimáticas*. This village inspired by ecological principles consists of 25 CO_2-neutral holiday homes. For a fascinating insight into current thinking, call in at the visitor centre *(Polígono Industrial de Granadilla s/n, Granadilla de Abona, http://casas.iter.es, photo)*. Not quite so ultra-modern, in fact the *Finca Constanza* is quite down-to-earth – bricks and old-fashioned iron railings in front of the window create a traditional look, but a water treatment system and a fragrant flower and vegetable garden adjust the environmental balance *(Adeje, www.finca-constanza.de)*. At the heart of a protected area is the *Eco Resort Sandos San Blas*. This well-designed eco-resort also runs a number of educational courses, including an introduction to medicinal herbs and an archaeology workshop *(Chafiras Carretera General, Los Abrigo, www.sanblas.eu)*.

Trail running

Uphill and down dale Jogging is so boring; try cross-country instead. It's best to start on Tenerife's *Blue Trail*, which crosses the entire island *(www.tenerifebluetrail.com)*. The annual 'Tenerife Bluetrail' race is based on the principle of 'trail running for all', so runners of varying abilities take part in one marathon race with trails of different lengths. If you would like to know more, enquire at *CAV Tenerife*, a body which organises races and competitions on the island *(www.cavtenerife.com)*. Shoes and equipment available from *Tenerife Outdoor (Avenida de Abona Mencey 49, Granadilla de Abona)*.

IN A NUTSHELL

ARCHITECTURE

One distinctive feature of traditional Canarian architecture is the lavish ornamentation on the woodwork, both internally and externally. Elaborately carved balconies, bay windows, arcades and staircases appear on many facades. Closely latticed shutters allow the air to circulate, but they also exclude the sun, creating an air-conditioning effect. In contrast, the whitewashed facades are strikingly simple. House corners cut from blocks of rough volcanic stone and pale red roof tiles reveal strong contrasts. The hub of a house is the *patio*, the inner courtyard, which provides access to all the rooms through arcades on each floor. There will often be luxurious plantings, there might even be a fountain, but the intention is to create a cool, green retreat from the warm Canarian climate. La Orotava and La Laguna showcase the best examples of Canarian architecture. Churches and town houses have carved and finely painted timber ceilings inside, often in Moorish-inspired mudéjar style. Outside, the prevailing style is classic colonial: white facades, window and door frames in natural stone and huge, often ornamented portals. The best preserved mountain village in Tenerife is Masca, where the houses are dry stone walled, i.e. no mortar.

THE ARTS

In earlier times, if you lived on the Canaries and wanted to express yourself through art, then you quickly headed

Of Guanches and dragon trees – Tenerife has much more to offer than just sunshine, beaches and the Pico del Teide

off to the European mainland, leaving behind the artistic desert on the islands. This was true for many years of the 20th century, when Franco's dictatorship stifled any non-conformism. But one *tinerfeño* artist did succeed in bringing back to the Atlantic island much of what he had learned while living in Paris among Picasso's contemporaries. In 1935 Óscar Domínguez, and none other than André Breton, organised a major Surrealism exhibition in Tenerife's capital, thus bringing to this distant Atlantic province

avant-garde art from all over the world – nothing like that had ever happened before. His artistic awakening was brought to an abrupt end by the Spanish Civil War (1936–39) and Domínguez remained in exile in France until he committed suicide in 1957. However, at the very least, he created the basis for later artistic activities.

Today there is not only a permanent exhibition of Domínguez' works in the prestigious *Tenerife Espacio de Arte (TEA)*, but also in several other reputable galleries, e.g. the *Galería Leyendecker (Rambla 86 | www.leyendecker.net),* and the *El Tanque* cultural centre *(Calle 70)* in Santa Cruz, the *Fundación Cristino de Vera* and the *Sala Conca* in La Laguna. The works of many modern artists are also often shown in temporary exhibitions at the *MACEW (Casa de Aduana | Calle Las Lonjas s/n)* in Puerto de la Cruz's former customs house above the tourist information office,

Art fans will also appreciate the extensive collection of art books and catalogues in the *Galería Biblioteca Expresión Contemporánea Antonin Artaud (Calle Estrecha 5)* in San Juan de la Rambla near Puerto de la Cruz. Then there's the *Finca de Arte* above Los Cristianos *(Chayofa | Calle Centro | www.finca-del-arte.com),* a popular

meeting place for international artists who have settled in Tenerife. The most important art event staged on Tenerife today is the *Foto Noviembre* (odd-numbered years only), where selected exhibits from recent photographic projects elsewhere in the world are on display *(www.fotonoviembre.com).*

THE CANARY

Its plumage is yellow, its song melodic. It usually sits in a cage and warbles to the delight of its owner. Even in the remotest corners of the world, it is just as much at home in a hut as in a palace. Many people are familiar with the yellow-green bird, but they may not know that it is also the name of an archipelago in the Atlantic.

Dragon trees such as this magnificent specimen in Los Realejos can grow to a height of 20m

The canary is a relative of the wild *Serenus canaria*, a bird which still inhabits the archipelago's forests. It does sing beautifully, but its appearance is not so spectacular. Over the years its plumage was modified through selective breeding, until it acquired its present colour.

CARNAVAL

No-one thinks of Tenerife when, every year, footage of the colourful Brazilian carnivals appears on television. But the exuberant spectacle on this Canary Island easily bears comparison with Rio's samba party. Months of preparatory work are needed for the wild weeks in February and March, *Carrozas* or floats have to be built and decorated, costumes must be sewn, masks and disguises carefully crafted. *Murgas*, groups dressed in colourful jester-like costumes, compete with one another to make the best outfits, to sing the cheekiest songs and to play the weirdest music. During the *desfiles*, the processions, they dance and frolic noisily through the streets. In Santa Cruz de Tenerife alone there can be tens of thousands of revellers on the move, forming a heaving sea of bodies. Following on every night after these parades, which are transmitted live on national Spanish television, is a *mogollón*: a street party where the younger generation dance all night to vibrant Latin rhythms. And it goes on for days, if not weeks.

The official climax is the election of the *Reina del Carnaval*. It is not beauty that determines who is crowned as carnival queen, but the grace with which she manages to carry the extravagant costume – itself worth as much as a mid-range car and weighing only a little less. The children also have their own parade and their own queen.

The grand finale for the *carnaval* is the *Entierro de la Sardina*, the burial of the sardine. Once again there is a spectacular parade, but this time a huge cardboard sardine is dragged through the streets. It ends with a pyrotechnic explosion of Roman candles, rockets and firecrackers. Holidaymakers are encouraged to take part in all events. Ask at the tourist information offices for details.

DRAGO

No plant has captured the imagination of the Canary islanders quite so much as the dragon tree. This relative of the yucca, and a member of the lily family, became extinct beyond the Macaronesian islands (Canaries, Madeira, Azores, Cape Verde) 20 million years ago, although close relatives do exist in Africa and Asia.

In 1799 the German naturalist and explorer, Alexander von Humboldt, drew the oldest *drago* in the archipelago – it is still alive today in Icod de los Vinos and is reckoned to be over 500 years old. He puzzled over its origins, which he assumed must be somewhere in Asia. The Guanches regarded the tree as sacred, largely because of its resin, known as 'dragon's blood'. Strangely, it turns dark red when exposed to the air and in the distant past was used in the preparation of medicinal potions and ointments. If you cut a branch from the drago, it grows back as quickly as 'the head of a dragon'. That is why the early naturalists gave the tree its fairytale-inspired botanical name *Dracaena drago*. And the locals still revere their dragon trees. Every flower garden simply has to have one. Pictures of them appear on paintings, stamps and coins.

THE GUANCHES

Little is known about the island's original inhabitants, whose name translates as 'sons of Tenerife'. They colonised the archipelago from the 3rd century BC, arriving in several waves. It is thought they are related to the light-skinned Berbers of North Africa. This theory is supported by a significant discovery made in 1992: a stone inscribed with the characters *zanata*, which is the

The Europeans subjugated, enslaved or killed the natives. However, the survivors were quickly integrated into the colonist community. Their legacy can be seen in the Museo del Hombre y la Naturaleza in Santa Cruz, in the Museo Arqueológico in Puerto de la Cruz and also in the mysterious Pirámides de Güímar.

Snow on the sunshine island – take the cable car up to the winter wonderland of Teide National Park

name of a Berber tribe. More recent genetic research suggests they may have migrated from the Mediterranean basin around Sicily.

The Guanches were primarily farmers who reared goats and sheep. When the Spanish settlers arrived on the Canaries, Tenerife was divided into nine kingdoms, menceyatos, each one ruled by a mencey. Larger-than-life bronze statues of the Guanche kings line the promenade above the Plaza Patrona de Canarias in Candelaria. The Guanches lived mostly in caves, where they buried their mummified dead.

LUCHA CANARIA

Lucha canaria, Canarian wrestling, dates from the time of the Guanches. Twelve contestants in two teams compete in pairs against each other in a sand-lined ring about 15m in diameter. In a clearly defined face-to-face starting position they lean forward and attempt to grab the rolled-up trouser leg of the opponent with their left hand. In no more than three minutes the *luchadores* must try, using different grips, to throw their opponent to the ground. If you floor your opponent twice, you win. And then the team with the most victories wins the contest. *Lucha canaria* is unique to the Canary Islands and is in no way aimed at the tourist market. If you would like to watch a match, enquire at the tourist information office about fixtures; every major town has its own arena *(terrero de lucha canaria)*.

SNOW

It's only 300km (180 miles) to the Sahara Desert – so can it really snow it here? It can, and it does. Much of the *Parque Nacional de las Cañadas del Teide* is higher than 2,000m. In winter the mountain often has a white tip, but the surrounding sea of lava only rarely sees snow. Temperatures of 5°C below zero are not uncommon. It snow does fall, the daily newspapers will always make much of the event. And then one thing is certain: the following weekend many hundreds of warmly-wrapped Canary islanders will make the trek to the top in order to enjoy the white stuff.

The snow and ice on Mount Teide played an important commercial role at the time of the Spanish conquest. A new occupation, the ice vendors or los *neveros*, emerged. They earned a living from first making the dangerous ascent on foot to the top of Teide, then transporting the cold cargo, either on beasts of burden or on their backs, down into the villages and selling it.

VIRGEN DE CANDELARIA

At least a century before the arrival of the Spaniards, two Guanche goatherds found a Gothic statue of the Madonna and Child, which had been washed ashore near Candelaria. Legend has it that the fearful shepherds wanted to destroy it with stones, but their arms became paralysed as they started to throw. Clearly impressed by the figure's magical powers, the aboriginal Canar-

ians transported the figure into a cave and began to worship it. Later on, when Catholic missionaries arrived on the island, they used this belief in miracles to convert the Guanches. The statue was given the name *Our Lady of Candelaria* and a small church was built there in her honour. However in 1826, a freak wave washed the church and the Madonna out to sea. The present statue was made in 1827 by a local artist. The Virgin's complexion, as well as that of the child, is almost as black as the volcanic sand on the beach below the basilica.

WATER

There has to be a downside if the sun always shines: a shortage of water. In earlier times, there were many rivers on Tenerife and the dense pine and laurel forests absorbed the moisture from the trade winds. Wells and shafts, known as galleries, were driven deep into the mountains, reaching underground water supplies and this kept the farmers' crops irrigated. But since then, most of the trees have been felled and many of the wells have run dry. Rainwater is collected in some reservoirs. But it is mainly seawater desalination plants that supply the holiday resorts of Tenerife; there are also nine golf courses that need a lot of water. And water obtained in this way requires money and energy, mainly oil. The cost is high in both financial and environmental terms. Newer plants are being converted to the more acceptable reverse osmosis procedure, whereby the salt is mechanically removed from the seawater. It is forced through a semi-permeable membrane, which lets through the water molecules, but blocks the larger salt particles. Although tourism uses only about ten percent of the water – agriculture takes the lion's share, about 70 percent – please try to use it sparingly.

FOOD & DRINK

For many centuries the staple food on the Canary Islands was *gofio*, a flour made from roasted maize, millet or barley grains, in desperate times even grass seeds. Cultivating the cereal was simple; it could even be grown on terraced fields in the mountains.

Wherever water gushed through the gorges, millstones ground flour. This yellow or light brown powder was a filling, protein-rich food and best of all, it was always available and very versatile. In addition, it was flavour-neutral, so it mixed well with other ingredients. The Guanches conjured up bread and soups from *gofio*. If you see *gofio escaldado*, a *caldo* (broth) made with thickened gofio flour, then do give it a try. Now innovative chefs even mix finely ground ● *gofio*

with ice cream and banana purée – for daring, but still very tasty creations.

Soups and stews are very popular. Freshly-prepared *sopas* are served at almost every restaurant that specialises in local cuisine. One worthy of recommendation is the *potaje canario*, a hearty vegetable soup. *Potaje de cardos* is a peasant soup made from the fresh shoots of the wild thistle, which grows on the upland meadows.

For tinerfeños survival depended on the optimum use of the available resources. They tended sheep and goats and later on began to hunt rabbits. But meat and fish remained a luxury that, until the 20th century, few islanders could afford. Before the era of refrigeration, to protect against spoilage, animal produce had to be stored in brine or dried.

Gofio, mojo and bienmesabe – borne out of poverty, Canarian cuisine combines simplicity with ingenuity

So the islanders developed a speciality known as *adobos*. Food was marinated for weeks, sometimes months, in hot sauces made from oil, vinegar, bay leaf, herbs, garlic and pepper; only then did its typical flavour develop. There were no leftovers at the preparation stage. Everything went into the pot and dishes with curious names such as *ropa vieja* emerged – in English it means ‚old clothes', referring with delightful clarity to the recycled ingredients it contained. *Ropa vieja*, *puchero* and *rancho canario*, meat and vegetable stews, are now, of course, freshly prepared with pork, chick peas, potatoes, pasta, onions, saffron, garlic and spicy *chorizo* sausage. These are among the tastiest – and most traditional – dishes Tenerife's cuisine has to offer. So over the generations, Canarian cuisine developed its own character.

The traditional accompaniment are *papas arrugadas*, now a snack much-loved by tourists. The famous ‚wrinkly potatoes' are served in every restaurant. They are a special variety: small, dark on the out-

LOCAL SPECIALITIES

▶ **baifito en adobo** – marinated kid is eaten with salad and *papas*

▶ **bienmesabe** – translates as 'it tastes good to me' – a sticky, golden-brown dessert made with honey, almonds, egg yolks and lemon (photo right)

▶ **caldo de pescado** – a thin fish soup with potatoes and herbs

▶ **carajacas** – calves', pigs' or chicken liver chopped into pieces and pickled

▶ **cherne al cilantro** – pan-fried Canarian gilthead bream in coriander sauce

▶ **conejo en salmorejo** – rabbit in a marinade of bay leaves, garlic and wine

▶ **gofio escaldado** – gofio, thickened with a broth of *caldo de pescado* into a creamy, maize-yellow porridge, with herbs and paprika to taste

▶ **mojo rojo** – velvety to runny hot sauce of red chillies, oil, garlic, vinegar and salt. Accompanies meat dishes and *papas arrugadas*

▶ **mojo verde** – like *mojo rojo*, but green instead of red chillies and lots of parsley. Served with fish and *papas arrugadas*

▶ **papas arrugadas** – Canarian potatoes boiled in brine, always eaten with its wrinkly (in Spanish: *arrugado*) skin (photo left)

▶ **pella** – bread-like dough made from *gofio*, water and salt. Eaten sliced with *sancocho canario*

▶ **potaje canario** – thick soup of chickpeas, potatoes, seasonal vegetables and maize

▶ **potaje de berros** – mild watercress stew with bacon, potatoes, pumpkin, maize, yams. Gofio is then stirred in

▶ **rancho canario** – stew of chickpeas, potatoes, pork, noodles, onions, garlic, *chorizo*

▶ **ropa vieja** – thick stew of chickpeas, meat, vegetables and potatoes

▶ **sancocho canario** – salted fish, boiled and then eaten with vegetables, *mojo* and *pella*

side, yellow inside. Accompanying the potatoes is another delicacy that many will be familiar with, *mojo*. This spicy sauce – it could be red or green – comes with practically every dish.

Fish and seafood now dominate Tenerife's menus. Historically, that's illogical, given that the Guanches were rather poor fishermen. Nowadays cooking methods mainly reflect the ways of Spanish immigrants. *Vieja, cherne, sama, caballa, bocinegro* taste best a *la plancha*, which means fried with a little oil on a hot metal plate. These are all rather firm Canarian fish, which reveal their full flavour when served with a salad and *mojo*. Also very much in demand are *pulpo* and *choco*, two types of squid.

Cocina casera, today's typical Canarian fare, consists of an eclectic mix of dishes from all over the world: fennel from Andalusia, yams from Africa, saffron from La Mancha, stodgy desserts from England, pasta from Italy and chayote from Venezuela. These dishes are a reminder of the fact that for 400 years the Canary Islands were at the hub of three continents.

To round off a good meal without a dessert would be a criminal offence. In addition to practically every kind of fruit – bananas, oranges and apricots to papayas, guavas and mangoes, all of which are harvested on the island – comes *flan*, a caramel custard and now a very popular dessert. However, the highlight of any Canarian dessert menu has to be *bienmesabe*, a blend of honey, lime or lemon, almonds and eggs. Every meal has to be rounded off with a *cortado* or a *solo* — an espresso with or without milk.

With their meal, the locals will drink Tenerife's slightly bitter keg beer, Dorado, or a bottle of the island's wine. Among all the islands in the archipelago, Tenerife is the main wine producer and, in fact, has a long tradition with the fruit of the vine. Cultivation started shortly after the Conquest, and before long many barrels of locally-produced wine were finding their way to the European mainland. But the colonial rivalry between Spain and England destroyed what was a thriving trade. Phylloxera infestation caused further damage to the island's wine industry. The tide turned only af-

ter Spain joined the EU; money from Brussels was invested in agriculture and the tinerfeños began to rediscover their vine-growing expertise. Family wineries were modernised, new bodegas were

White or red – Tenerife's vintages are much sought after

opened and before long wines from Tenerife were winning international prizes. Today on Tenerife there are five different *Denominaciones de Origen* (Protected Designation of Origin). Grapes are harvested in September, so that the young wine can start to flow at Martinmas in early November – the wine festivals then continue in Icod de los Vinos, Puerto de la Cruz and Tacoronte. The best place to taste the island's vintages is the ● *Casa del Vino* in El Sauzal, just north of Puerto de la Cruz. For a small outlay, you can sample several different varieties.

SHOPPING

When it comes to shopping, the locals invariably choose Santa Cruz, because it boasts a well-stocked department store, namely El Corte Inglés, as well as many smart boutiques. For food and drink, the farmers' markets *(mercadillos de agricultor)* are the automatic choice. These are held at weekends, notably in Adeje and in Tacoronte.

For traditional handicrafts, of which you will find a wide choice on Tenerife, La Orotava is by far the best place – a walk through the Old Town is like a journey back in time. Beautifully carved balconies and arcades attest to the superior craftsmanship of Canarian woodcarvers. And even behind the facades the old traditions are maintained. For La Orotava is the centre of Tenerife's *artesanía*. Canarian craftsmanship goes back to the Guanche era and finds its strongest expression in a style of pottery typical of the archipelago. Original tinerfeño crafts come supplied with a guarantee and the manufacturer's name when you buy in the shops belonging to the state Artenerife chain, which also ensures that the artisans are fairly rewarded. They are to be found in Santa Cruz, Puerto de la Cruz, La Orotava, Playa de las Américas and Los Cristianos. *www.artenerife.com*

EMBROIDERY

Canarian embroidery, particularly the open threadwork style, has a long tradition on Tenerife; it is of outstanding quality, but the real thing comes at a price. With this type of sewing, material, stretched tightly on a wooden frame, is partially unravelled and then, using a complicated hemstitching technique *(calado)*, patterns or motifs, such as suns or roses, stitched on. The finished items are sold as tablecloths, table mats and handkerchiefs.

FOOD & DRINK

The best souvenir for friends and family back home is nearly always something to eat or drink. And here the Canary Islands can offer a great selection – cheese from happy goats, the delicious *bienmesabe* dessert, liqueurs made from palm juice or bananas and locally-made cakes and pastries. *Gofio*, the flour of the native Guanches, can be bought in many supermarkets. Or it can be bought directly from the miller at one of Tenerife's last working flour mills in La Orotava. You will need to find *Calle Doctor Domingo González García 3 (Mon–Fri 8am–1pm and 3pm–7pm, Sat 8am–1pm)*. Teobaldo Méndez has won many awards

Souvenirs in clay and cloth – hand-made crafts in all colours, shapes and sizes

for his delicious treats. In his shop, *El Aderno* in Buenavista del Norte, the best pâtissier on Tenerife sells traditional Canarian pastries, such as *rosquetes, truchas* and *merengues*. Teobaldo's secret is no surprise: he uses only the best ingredients. *Every day 9am–9pm | La Alhóndiga 8 | www.eladerno.com*

Tenerife's wines are among the best in the Canaries. Grape varieties, such as *listán blanco, listán negra* and *negramoll*, which produce light, dry wines, are grown at altitudes of up to 1,600m (5,250ft), mainly in the northwest. 'Frontos', a white wine produced from organically grown grapes in the Abona region, is currently enjoying plaudits from wine connoisseurs. Other wines from the island are available in bodegas, wine stores and good supermarkets.

FLOWERS

One delightful souvenir is the exotic bird of paradise plant (strelitzia), which is cultivated on Tenerife. On weekdays until noon, wom-

en from the villages sell these and many other flowers at the *Mercado de Flores* in Puerto de la Cruz. *Mon–Sat | Calle Santo Domingo*

POTTERY

Alfarería – bowls, plates, jugs and drinking vessels – were essential commodities for everyday life and would be produced with no particular artistic ambitions. Today it is their sheer simplicity that gives them their special appeal. In addition to La Orotava, where Canarian pottery is sold in the *Museo de Cerámica*, in many galleries and other shops, it is in the village of Arguayo near Santiago del Teide that the finest examples are made. Before buying, check carefully for authenticity.

WICKERWORK

The *cestería* is a useful, hand-crafted item. The baskets are made from cane, straw, and the fibres of palm leaves, skilfully spliced and woven together by the craft workers.

THE PERFECT ROUTE

FERTILE ISLAND

Start in ① *Puerto de la Cruz* → p. 44 and pass through the densely populated coastal region towards La Orotava. From the road the view is mainly of banana plantations. A string of villages line the ② *Valle de la Orotava* → p. 41. Bordered on both sides by steep hillsides, the valley climbs rapidly towards the centre of the island. The small town of ③ *La Orotava* → p. 40 (photo left) gets the benefit of the fresh mountain air, plus it enjoys fine views over the green valley, the blue sea and the white tip of Mount Teide. Romantic plazas, churches and monasteries serve as reminders of the island's colonial past.

INTO THE CRATER

A few metres away from the TF-21 above the 16 km marker, near Aguamansa lies the green crater of ④ *La Caldera* → p. 44 – now a picnic area. Tours depart from a dense forest of Canary Island pines that filter the water from the clouds through their long needles. Between the 22 and 23 km markers, stop to take a look at La Margarita de Piedra (Stone Rose), a large basalt rosette, the exposed remains of a volcanic tunnel.

IN THE PARK

At an altitude of 2,000m the forest thins and volcanic rock predominates. El Portillo, an attractive visitor centre, forms the gateway to the ⑤ *National Park* → p. 68 (photo right). A rock garden here contains all the plants that have adapted to the extreme climate; by far the finest is the Mount Teide bugloss, a herbaceous perennial that grows to a height of about 2m and sports a mass of reddish flowers in late spring or early summer.

ON THE MOUNTAIN

As the road continues, the vista varies between lava and ash fields, which shimmer in white, green, red, grey and pitch black. They bear witness to the volcanic activity, which shaped the land millions of years ago. Do take the cable car up ⑥ *Mount Teide* → p. 70, which at 3,718m (12,198ft) is the highest mountain in Spain. In the winter it often wears a white snow cap.

GREAT VIEWS

The ⑦ *Roques de García* → p. 70 are giant weathered rock formations that tower above a crater framed by jagged cliffs. The nearby Parador with cafeteria is the per-

Get to see the many different sides of Tenerife along the north coast and inland – and include a cable car ride up Mount Teide

fect place to break your journey. Next door, a visitor centre provides information about other aspects of the National Park. The following make spectacular vantage points: first there's the 5-m high Zapato de la Reina (Queen's Shoe), then comes the Boca de Tauce, a breach in the caldera rim, and finally the Mirador de Chío. Looking across fields of black clinker, you will see the **8** *Pico Viejo → p. 70*, Mount Teide's younger brother.

A CITY STROLL

On the return journey from **9** *El Portillo → p. 71* take the TF-24 across the island's backbone to La Laguna. Around the 32 km marker, you will pass several black-white grey rock formations that clearly show the compressed layers of volcanic rock. After that you are back in pine forest. Where the woodland thins out, you will find a series of viewpoints. Sometimes you look east, sometimes northwest, sometimes you see the neighbouring island of La Palma, sometimes Gran Canaria.

10 *La Laguna → p. 54*, a Unesco World Heritage site, is a picture-book town with cobbled, pedestrianised streets lined by monasteries and elegant mansions.

TO THE BEACH

From La Laguna, take the TF-5 motorway to Puerto de la Cruz and enjoy an early evening swim. The pitch black **11** *Playa Jardín → p. 49* at Puerto de la Cruz is the perfect place for a refreshing dip after a day's sightseeing. Then relax over a refreshing cocktail in one of the palm-shaded beach bars.

105km (65 miles). Driving time: 3 hours. Detailed map of the route on the back cover, in the road atlas and the pull-out map

THE
NORTHWEST

Nowhere else on Tenerife is the landscape more varied than in the northwest. The Valle de la Orotava is the green, fertile heart of the island. At one time this broad valley was the main settlement area for the Guanches and the Spanish conquerors also preferred this bounteous region. First wine, then sugar cane and finally the banana brought prosperity to landowners.

When he first set eyes on the valley in 1799, Alexander von Humboldt is said to have fallen to his knees to thank God for creating this paradise. He later wrote: '... I have never beheld a prospect more varied, more attractive, more harmonious in the distribution of the masses of verdure and rocks than the western coast of Tenerife.' A look-out point, the ● *Mi-rador de Humboldt* has been created in his memory at the very spot where he surveyed the valley for the first time. Today, despite modest beaches and steep cliffs, tourism is the most important source of income. Boxy hotel blocks line the coastal zone around Puerto de la Cruz, the regional centre for the north of Tenerife. The further west you go, the more you put the tourist throng behind you. In small villages, farmers tend their crops, keep goats or cultivate vines, in much the same way as they have done for centuries, but always with an eye on Mount Teide looming behind them to the south. Stretching out beyond the town of Garachico are the rugged and largely uninhabited Teno Mountains. Until a few years ago the only human habita-

Photo: Buenavista del Norte

A region of contrasts – cultural heritage sites and holiday centres, barren volcanic slopes and lush vegetation

tion was in remote villages trapped in an almost medieval existence.

GARACHICO

(133 D2) (∅ D5) ⭐ ☼ **When you leave the Teno Mountains, you will find yourself looking down on one of the most beautiful places on the island – Garachico, with a population of about 5,700 has the feel of a warm and friendly village.** Until its destruction by the eruption of the Montaña Negra in 1706 – traces of it can still seen on the mountain slopes behind Garachico – this town was Tenerife's leading port. But streams of lava flowed down across a broad front to the northwest and formed the *Isla Baja*, the 'low island' on which Garachico now stands, just east of the two villages of Los Silos and Buenavista del Norte. The inhabitants defiantly rebuilt their town on the only recently cooled lava.

Visitors enjoy taking a stroll through the Old Town, where buildings, which miraculously survived the destruction, create what is a living museum. On the elevated *Plaza de la Libertad* opposite the church stands a memorial statue to the Venezuelan national hero, Simon Bolivar, whose grandmother emigrated to the New World from Garachico.

SIGHTSEEING

CASTILLO DE SAN MIGUEL
One of the few structures to survive the disaster of 1706 unscathed was San Miguel castle, which was built in 1575. The tiny fortification was once owned by the Counts of Gomera. Several coats of arms adorn the massive portal. Inside there is a small collection of natural history artefacts. *Mon–Sat 10am–3.30pm | Admission 1 euro | Avenida Tome Cano s/n*

CONVENTO DE SAN FRANCISCO
The convent dating from 1524 and its church with high wooden ceilings in mudéjar style are the oldest surviving buildings in Garachico. Impressive features in the monastery wing are the large cloister with an all-round gallery and fine woodwork, columns and filigree stone flooring. The *Casa de la Cultura* is also housed here. Attached to it is a low-key natural history museum with a collection of fossils. Probably of more interest are the exhibitions about volcanic activity, including a scale model of island, on which all past eruptions are marked. Upstairs, more displays put local volcanic activity in a global context and a series of multimedia installations provide greater clarity. *Mon–Fri 11am–2pm and 3.30pm–6.30pm, Sat 10am–3pm | Admission 1 euro | Plaza de la Libertad*

IGLESIA DE SANTA ANA
Dating originally from 1520, the church was rebuilt after it was destroyed in 1706. Flanking the classical tabernacle are the figures of Santa Ana and San Joaquin (18th century), both works by the great Canarian sculptor, Luján Pérez.

MUSEO DE ARTE CONTEMPORANEO
Housed in the church belonging to the former monastery of Santo Domingo is the Museum of Contemporary Art, which showcases the work of mainly Spanish artists in temporary exhibitions. *Open at irregular times | Admission 1 euro | Convento de Santo Domingo*

FOOD & DRINK

EL CALETÓN ☼
Surrounded by volcanic rocks below the promenade is a terraced restaurant, where guests can sit and watch the breaking waves. The view is great, the fast food disappointing – best if you just order a drink! *Daily | Tel. 9 22 13 33 01 | Moderate*

CASA GASPAR
Even after the move, the Gaspar still has a lot to commend it – meat from the grill and fresh fish, costed by weight, fast and friendly service. *Closed Sun, Mon | Calle*

Garachico is rightly considered to be one of the most beautiful towns on the island

Esteban del Ponte 44 | tel. 9 22 83 00 40 | Moderate

SHOPPING

CENTRO ARTESANÍA EL LIMONERO

This shop by the harbour promenade sells a lot of knick-knacks, but you can buy some interesting regional speciali- ties here, e.g. cheese and wine. *Mon–Sat 10.30am–8.30pm, Sun 11am–7pm | Ave- nida Tomé Cano s/n*

WHERE TO STAY

INSIDER TIP LA QUINTA ROJA

This delightful country hotel with a fine patio occupies a renovated 17th-century manor house. Twenty rooms with lots of wood. Roof terrace with jacuzzi and sau- na. Good value for money. Restaurant, cafeteria and tasca (wine bar) open to non-residents. *Glorieta de San Francisco s/n | tel. 9 22 13 33 77 | www.quintaroja. com | Moderate*

MARCO POLO HIGHLIGHTS

★ **Garachico**
Historic Old Town, wild and wind- swept coast, a castle and nice restaurants → p. 33

★ **San Roque**
This elegant hotel is situated in the centre of Garachico → p. 36

★ **Masca**
A picturesque natural stone vil- lage in the heart of the Teno mountains → p. 36

★ **Drago Milenario**
Icod de los Vinos – home to what is the oldest dragon tree in the world → p. 38

★ **Casas de los Balcones**
Admire La Orotava's grand houses with delightful patios → p. 41

★ **Jardín Botánico**
You will be bowled over by the ex- otic trees and flowers in Puerto de la Cruz's Botanical Garden → p. 46

SAN ROQUE ⭐

A jewel in the crown of the Canarian hotel trade – this 17th-century mansion has been furnished with great attention to detail. All 20 rooms fitted out with designer furniture. Pool and terrace, not to mention the romantic leafy patio, create the perfect holiday atmosphere. *Calle Esteban de Ponte 32 | tel. 9 22 13 34 35 | www.hotelsanroque.com | Expensive*

WHERE TO GO

BUENAVISTA DEL NORTE
(132 B2) (*ᗰ C5*)

Only 10km (7 miles) from Garachico lies Tenerife's most westerly town (pop. 5,400). Towering up behind it the impressive Teno Mountains. The TF-445 heads west to *Buenavista Golf*, an 18-hole golf course sloping down to the sea with a palatial five-star hotel *(Vincci Buena Vista Golf & Spa | 117 rooms | Calle La Finca s/n | tel. 9 22 06 17 00 | www.vinccihoteles.com | Expensive | Golf: tel. 9 22 12 90 34 | Green fee: 1 round 75 euros | www.tenerifegolf.es)*.

Continue on the TF-445 past the �r☀ *Mirador de Don Pompeyo*, with a fine long-distance view, before it ends (risk of landslide if wet and windy) at the ☀ *Punta de Teno*. An old lighthouse stands alongside the new one. On clear days the view extends as far as La Palma and La Gomera.

MACIZO DE TENO (TENO MOUNTAINS)
(132 B–C 3–4) (*ᗰ B–C6*)

Like the Anaga Mountains in the northeast of Tenerife, the *Macizo de Teno* in the northwest is rugged and inaccessible mountain terrain, which rises to a height of 1,100m (3,500ft). Geologically it is one of the oldest parts of the island. Rising up out of the sea to form an island about 7 million years ago, it is traversed by steep gorges, terrain that is extremely inhospitable for human habitation. For centuries, the few villages here were practically cut off from the outside world. But in the early 1990s, an asphalt road, parts of which are still quite demanding for drivers, leads to this secluded corner of the island. The ☀ *Mirador de Cherfe* on the road from Santiago del Teide to Masca is a great vantage point.

If you love this wild, unspoilt terrain, keep going and then just south of El Palmar turn to the west toward *Teno Alto* (132 B3) (*ᗰ B6*). Every first and third Sunday in the month a INSIDER TIP small farmer's market is held at this junction. Continue toward Teno Alto passing a picnic site and then after 3km (2 miles), you will reach this remote hamlet dispersed across a windswept upland plateau. Grazing on the pastures around Teno Alto are goats and sheep, whose milk is processed into a 🕐 cheese, which frequently wins awards. You can sample it in the bars on the church square, ideally with a glass of wine. The Macizo de Teno is *Parque Natural* and so is a protected area.

MASCA ⭐ ☀ (132 B–C4) (*ᗰ C6–7*)

Masca, situated some 21km (13 miles) south of Garachico, is a fascinating village, but even when you are quite close, you will barely notice it. The houses, spread across the hillsides, were built with blocks of stone hewn from the grey-brown rock found in the surrounding area. This architectural style is typical of the Teno region and Masca is the best example. The oldest building, the *Casa de los Avinculados*, is in the La Piedra district. Until well into the 20th century, ancient shepherd tracks created by the Guanches were the only link with the outside world. They wound along the mountain slopes from village to village as far as Santiago del Teide. A leisurely way to get to know Masca is to visit either early in the morning or later on in evening, when the place is not overrun by tourists on island coach tours. Below the main road you will find a number of 🍴 tourist cafes, with terracing overlooking the mountains and the valleys (e.g. *Casa Fidel | closed Thu | tel. 9 22 86 34 57 | Budget*).

A spectacular trail (3 hours) winds along the barranco down to the sea, but this trail is suitable only for fit, sure-footed hikers.

SANTIAGO DEL TEIDE (132 C4) (*ⓜ C7*)

In geographical terms, this rather nondescript place (pop. 5,400) belongs to the Teno Mountains. It is situated 17km (10 miles) south of Garachico on a plateau at an altitude of just over 900m (2,950ft). It is of interest only for its *Iglesia de San Fernando* topped by several white domes. Politically it is more important. The small town is in fact the administrative centre for several holiday settlements around Puerto de Santiago on the coast 10km (7 miles) away and so since the late 70s it has become much more prosperous.

Well worth a visit is the hamlet of *Arguayo* south of Santiago. It was once an important centre for Tenerife's pottery trade. Happily, the craft and the skills required live on in the INSIDER TIP ▶ *Museo del Alfarero*. The pottery museum is housed in a renovated workshop. Following the traditional Guanche method – i.e. no potter's wheel or tools – all ceramics are fired in an old oven. On sale here are the finished products, i.e. simple dishes, pots and pans in natural shades. The exhibits include some of the finest pieces the potters have produced and some old photographs from the days when business was

An exceptional walking trail – through the Masca gorge down to the sea

booming. *Tue–Sat 10am–1pm, 4pm–7pm, Sun 10am–2pm | Admission free*

LOS SILOS (132 C2) *(ﾉﾉ C5)*

Almost all of the residents in this town (pop. 5,500) 6km (4 miles) to west of Garachico live off the land. However, the first apartment blocks by the coast in the settlements of La Caleta and San José show that tourism also plays a part. Open-air pools right by the sea are the preferred option to stony beaches. The church of Nuestra Señora de la Luz (20th-century) in 'gingerbread' style by the pleasant plaza is the most important building. It houses the much-copied 17th-century statue known as the Cristo de la Misericordia, the Christ of Humility and Patience. Diagonally opposite the church in an old convent is a 🕐 *visitor centre*, which can supply helpful information on the local geology, flora and fauna, and walking opportunities in the Teno Mountains *(Centro de Visitantes | Plaza de la Luz 10 | Mon–Fri 9am–1pm, Sat 9am–2pm)*.

Walkers will find an excellent place to stay some 200m from the coast. The outdoor holiday tour operator, Wikinger, runs a four-star aparthotel INSIDER TIP *Luz del Mar* with large pool and spa. Guests will find here not only a wide choice of walking trails with detailed descriptions, but they will also have the opportunity to join in with (almost daily) guided tours. There are mountain bikes to hire and the centre also organises kayaking, caving and paragliding tours. In the evenings non-residents are welcome to eat in the adjoining *restaurant*, where there is a warm and friendly atmosphere. Many of the ingredients come from the 🕐 organic finca that belongs to the centre. *35 rooms, 14 suites | Av. Sibora 10 | La Caleta | tel. 9 22 84 16 23 | www. luzdelmar.de/englisch/st | Moderate*

EL TANQUE (133 D2) *(ﾉﾉ D5)*

In the *Camello Center* some 6km (4 miles) above Garachico a herd of dromedaries and some donkeys take visitors on rides through the surrounding area. *Daily 10am–5.30pm | 20 mins Camel ride 8 euros | Donkey ride 4 euros | TF-82*

ICOD DE LOS VINOS

(133 E2) *(ﾉﾉ E5)* It's named after a tree and every year thousands of visitors flock here to admire it. But bear in mind that the legendary dragon tree in Icod de los Vinos is the finest example of its kind on the island.

Although the ★ ● *Drago Milenario* does not date back a thousand years as the name suggests, its age is estimated at 500 to 600 years, and so must be the oldest dragon tree in the world. With an average trunk diameter of 6m (20ft) and a height of 17m (56ft), it is also unsurpassed in size. It occupies a prominent position in the middle of town within an enclosed garden, the *Parque del Drago*. The centre of the historic town of Icod (pop. 23,000) is worth exploring. Founded in 1501, it quickly acquired a reputation for its fertile vineyards. Many *bodegas* still line the streets and plazas of the Old Town, which throngs with pedestrians and cars.

SIGHTSEEING

IGLESIA SAN MARCOS & PLAZA DE PILA

Just a stone's throw away from the Drago Milenario stands the 15th-century *San Marcos* church with its impressive Renaissance portal. Of interest inside is the wooden ceiling carved from the Canarian pine and the Baroque altar decorated with embossed silver. In the Treasury there is a silver cross from Mexico. Next door is the slightly elevated *Plaza de Pila*, ringed by perfectly preserved town houses dating from the 18th century.

PARQUE DEL DRAGO

The park in which the dragon tree stands has in recent years been enlarged into a botanical garden with a collection of many native plants. One new feature is a Guanche trail, which sheds light on the lives of the island's aboriginal inhabitants. *Daily 9am–6pm | Admission 4 euros*

FOOD & DRINK

CARMEN

Near the San Marcos church is a rustic-style restaurant, well patronised by locals and serving a wide range of Canarian specialities: do try the traditional island stew, *potaje de berros. Closed Mon | Calle Hercules 2 | tel. 9 22 81 06 31 | Moderate*

WHERE TO STAY

CASABLANCA

This terraced estate dating from the 18th century lies in a protected gorge, the *Barranco de Ruiz*, at an altitude of 600m (1,950ft). The 20 rooms are stylishly decorated with terracotta and lots

A magnificent specimen – the drago milenario in Icod de los Vinos

of wood; there is also a restaurant and a pool garden. *Calle Real 16 | Icod El Alto | tel. 9 22 35 96 21 | www.hotelruralcasablanca.com | Moderate*

PIEDRA REDONDA

In the village of Icod you will find this 150-year-old, fully renovated and fully furnished house with two double bedrooms, living room, dining room, fireplace and terrace. Ideal for people who like to holiday independently. *Booking*

ICOD DE LOS VINOS

via Attur | tel. 9 02 21 55 82 | www.eco
turismocanarias.com | *Moderate*

WHERE TO GO

CUEVA DEL VIENTO ● (133 E3) (*Ⓜ E6*)

If you call in at the small visitor centre a
few kilometres southeast of Icod, first of
all you will receive an introduction into
how the 'Cave of the Wind' came into
being. It was formed about 27,000 years
ago, when the Pico Viejo erupted and sent
trails of lava flowing down into the valley.
The lava cooled rapidly at the surface,
while underneath it kept flowing, thereby
creating tunnels; at 17km (10 miles) in
length and three different levels, this is
the longest lava tube in the world. In what
is eternal darkness, only highly adaptable
creatures have been able to make a home
here, notably insects, such as the blind
cockroach (loboptera subterranea).
Only about 200m of the cave is open to
the public (hopefully it will be extended
to almost 2km), but even this small
section gives a good idea of the cave's
dimensions. *Cueva del Viento | Tue–Sat
9am–4pm | Admission 15 euros | Visits
three times per day in Spanish and Eng-
lish for small groups | Pre-booking es-
sential: tel. 9 22 81 53 39 | www.cueva
delviento.net | Sturdy shoes required*

SAN JUAN DE LA RAMBLA
(134 A2) (*Ⓜ F5*)

The elongated village (pop. 5,000) is located in an area of steep cliffs with inten-
sive banana cultivation. The plantations
continue into the heart of the village
In *Las Aguas,* the fishing quarter, there
is a fine sea water swimming pool. The
🍴 *Las Aguas* restaurant occupies a picturesque spot in a low-rise country house
above the promenade. Seafood is one of
its specialities. *Closed Mon | Calle Hercu-
les 20 | tel. 9 22 36 04 28 | Moderate*

SAN MARCOS (133 E2) (*Ⓜ E5*)

The INSIDER TIP *Playa de San Marcos*, in
a cove 2km north of Icod de los Vinos,
is very popular with the locals, but one
which few tourists know about. About
100m in length, the beach of pitch-black
volcanic sand is deserted on weekdays,
but on Saturday and Sunday it fills up
with hundreds of islanders, mainly
those taking weekend breaks in nearby
apartments; their trade keeps the small,
local restaurants busy. One of them, the
🍴 *Tasca el Muelle* is on the promenade
overlooking sea and beach. Their speciality – like almost everywhere else here
– is fish. *Daily | tel. 9 22 81 51 59 | Budget–
Moderate*

LA OROTAVA

(134 C2) (*Ⓜ H5*) **Grand town houses
line steep narrow lanes. Elegant mansions with spacious, dark-wood balconies surround large squares.**

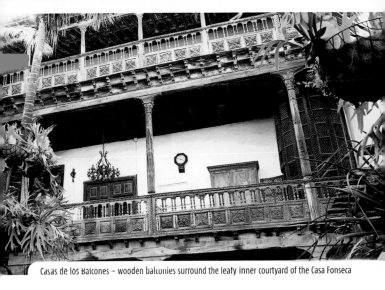

Casas de los Balcones – wooden balconies surround the leafy inner courtyard of the Casa Fonseca

The Guanches had a good reason for settling here. Before the Conquest water bubbled from the many springs on the hillsides in the green Valle de la Orotava, its fertile soil giving the first settlers grain and water. No wonder then that at the beginning of the 16th century the Spaniards decided to build a colonial town here – La Orotava. They planted sugar cane, which they then shipped from the port, Puerto de la Orotava (now: Puerto de la Cruz), all over the world, and in the process amassed considerable wealth.

Although earthquakes in 1704 and 1705 destroyed large parts of the town, they were immediately rebuilt. That explains why the historic core remains largely intact and has been spared the architectural monstrosities of modern times. It is rightly protected as a fine example of Europe's cultural heritage. The situation is rather different in the newer, outer suburbs, where congestion slows traffic. Tourism in La Orotava (pop. 40,000) is mainly restricted to day visitors.

SIGHTSEEING

CASAS DE LOS BALCONES ★

Several town houses of simple elegance face each other in *Calle San Francisco*. They get their name, *Casas de los Balcones*, from the wonderful finely turned wooden balconies, so typical of the Canaries. It's as if they have been stuck to the facade. The first, the *Casa Fonseca*, was built in 1632. What fascinates visitors is the tropical-green patio and an arcade panelled entirely with wood on the first floor. The rooms are now used by an embroidery school. On sale are blankets and fabrics, which you can watch being made. In 1670 the equally fine house next door, the *Casa de Franchi* was built; it now houses a *'carpet museum' (Museo de las Alfombras)*. However, these are not woven pieces, but floor coverings made from lava sand, as seen in the Corpus Christi celebrations. Opposite is *Casa Molina*, formerly a monastery dating from 1590. It now houses one of the island's largest craft shops. *www.casa-balcones.com*

HIJUELA DEL BOTÁNICO

Situated behind the town hall is the 0.4-heactare (1-acre) botanical garden, laid out in 1788 on the initiative of Count of Villanueva del Prado. Specimens of particular interest in the beautifuly manicured grounds include Australian conifers, Indian chestnut trees, flame trees and a very fine dragon tree. *Mon–Fri 8am–2pm| Admission free | Calle Tomás Pérez s/n*

JARDINES DE LA QUINTA DEL MARQUESADO ROJA

Beside the Plaza de la Constitución a park with neat lawns, flower beds in an extravagant array of colour climbs up a terraced slope. *Daily 9am–6pm | Admission free*

MUSEO DE ARTESANÍA-IBEROAMERICANA

Within the walls of the former Dominican monastery of Santo Domingo, which dates from the 17th century, is an arts and crafts museum. Exhibits include traditional costumes, instruments and handicrafts from Spain and the New World. The monastery's cloister is a masterpiece of simplicity. *Mon–Sat 9am–3pm | Admission 2.50 euros | Calle Tomás Zerolo 34*

PARROQUIA DE LA INMACULADA CONCEPCIÓN DE LA VIRGEN MARÍA

The splendour of the Baroque-style church dedicated to the Virgin of the Immaculate Conception is a testament to the town's importance. Work started on this house of worship in the early 16th Century, but it was destroyed by

Manicured gardens – the Jardines del Marquesado de la Quinta Roja in La Orotava

the earthquakes of 1704/05. The present church was consecrated in 1788 and declared a National Monument in 1948. Two graceful bell towers frame the massive facade. The three naves in the interior are separated by Ionic columns, above the chancel is a dome. Another interesting feature is the 1823 high altar of marble and jasper from the Genoese School. *Plaza Casañas s/n*

PLAZA DEL AYUNTAMIENTO

La Orotava's main square, overlooked by seven towering Canary palm trees, is in front of town hall. This is the stage for all the major festivals, including the colourful Corpus Christi celebrations. In the weeks before Christmas, the plaza is transformed into Tenerife's largest INSIDER TIP nativity scene.

PLAZA DE LA CONSTITUCIÓN ⚜

Constitution Square centred around the café pavilion forms the heart of La Orotava. It is generously proportioned and always beautifully planted with flowers and shrubs.

RUTA DE LOS MOLINOS DE AGUA

No fewer than nine waterwheels were built to take advantage of La Orotava's abundance of water. Although built in the 16th century, they continued in use until well into modern times. They stood one behind the other along streets that climbed steeply up the hillside, their job being to grind *gofio*, the Canarian staple food. All were linked by channels, which carried water from the Araujo river from one mill to another. Seven of the mills and parts of the channels can still be seen. One of the three still functioning mills – in the *Calle Domingo González García 3* – is now powered by electricity and continues to grind *gofio*, which you can buy locally. *Mon–Fri 8am–1pm and 3pm–7pm, Sat 8am–1pm | Start of route: south of the Casas de los Balcones*

SABOR CANARIO

The chefs in this rustic complex in the heart of La Orotava devote loving attention to traditional Canarian fare – from *rancho* to *bienmesabe. Daily | Calle Carrera 17 | tel. 9 22 32 27 25 | Budget–Moderate*

CASA DE LOS BALCONES AND CASA DEL TURISTA

As well as culinary specialities and tobacco products, the shops in the two houses opposite one another also sell *calados*, i.e. hemstitched embroidery, and *artesanía*, such as costumes, pottery and wood carvings. *Mon–Sat 9am–6.30pm (Casa de los Balcones, also Sun) | Calle San Fernando 3 and 4*

CASA TORREHERMOSA

Tenerife's arts and crafts chain, *Artenerife*, has its local outlet in a mansion, which dates from the 17th century. *Mon–Fri 10am–5pm, Sat 10am–1pm | Calle Tomás Zerolo 27*

INSIDER TIP LA PALOMA

This traditional village hotel in the heart of Old Town was built with dark volcanic stone. With lots of elegant wooden furnishings, two bedrooms, bathroom, kitchen and living room, it is let as one unit (for up to 5 persons). *Calle Salazar 23 | tel. 9 22 10 58 58 | www.casa-lapaloma. com | Budget*

SILENE

This simple guesthouse offers comfortable accommodation in a town house. Three of the four rooms have balconies overlooking the town. *Calle Tomás Zerolo 9 | tel. 9 22 33 01 99 | Budget*

VICTORIA

This beautiful, two-storey mansion dating from the 16th century is now a lovely hotel with 14 rooms. A tiled, rustically furnished patio serves as a lounge, the in-house restaurant serves delicious food. Plus bar, tasca and sun terrace. *Calle Hermano Apolinar 8 | tel. 9 22 33 16 83 | www.hotelruralvictoria.com | Moderate*

INFORMATION

OFICINA DE TURISMO

Calle Calvario | tel. 9 22 32 30 41 | www.villadelaorotava.org

WHERE TO GO

AGUAMANSA ☼

(134 C2) (ⓜ J5)

Beyond the village of Aguamansa, about halfway (10km/7 miles) between La Orotava and the Parque Nacional del Teide, there is a dense pine forest. That is a good enough reason to take a break and look back up the Orotava Valley. Drive past the *ICONA* centre in a house belonging to the National Park – where walkers will find a wealth of information – and you will find on the left-hand side the *La Caldera* picnic site in a volcanic crater. There are walking trails from Aguamansa to La Orotava and Los Realejos.

PUERTO DE LA CRUZ

 MAP INSIDE BACK COVER
(134 B–C 1–2) (*ⓜ G–H 4–5*) **Large apartment blocks and hotels surrounded by lush gardens, colourful adventure pools, a rather rundown port, grand colonial buildings alongside neon-lit bars, bustling shopping streets, one end a haunt for old men passing the time of day on shady squares – this is Puerto de la Cruz in a nutshell. It's been difficult finding the right balance between the past, present and future.**

By 1900 the British had discovered this cool spot and pleasant climate, and claimed it for themselves. The first hotels were built in spacious gardens above the fishing village, which until then had been used by the Spanish, mainly as a port for exporting sugar cane and wine from the Orotava Valley. There were elegant hotels like the Hotel Taoro, which still stands proudly above the city, but it desperately needs investment. Many Canary islanders only settled here once tourism had become established; since the 1960s the spa hotels have been joined by multi-storey tourist blocks and guesthouses.

Puerto de la Cruz's infrastructure is geared towards supplying services to and meeting the cultural needs of its 45,000 inhabitants as well as meeting the demands of the hundreds of thousands of holidaymakers who flock to the town. The locals and the world of tourism have to rub along together in this town, which has deep historic roots – that is what makes Puerto de la Cruz different from the resorts in the south. The best way to get a feel for the place is to take a stroll through the jumble of lanes in the Old Town – better to walk, than to drive into a web of one-way streets. Between the Playa de Martiánez in the east and the Plaza del Charco in the centre, you will find many shops and restaurants, squares to relax in, modern glass palaces as well as fine examples of colonial architecture.

Tue–Thu, Sat 10am–2pm, Fri 5pm–8pm | Calle Las Lonjas 1

CASTILLO SAN FELIPE

Situated west of the town centre just under 1km away is San Felipe castle. It was built between 1630 and 1644 to defend

Today art and culture dominate behind the thick walls of the Castillo San Felipe

SIGHTSEEING

CASA DE LA REAL ADUANA

One of the oldest buildings in Puerto de la Cruz is the Royal Customs House. Built in 1620, its wooden windows and balconies perfectly exemplify Canarian architecture. The last customs formalities were completed 150 years ago. Now the ground floor of the building houses the tourist office, an *Artenerife* shop selling handicrafts, kitchenware and local delicacies, while on display upstairs in the *Museum of Contemporary Art (MACEW)* are changing exhibitions of works by Canarian and other Spanish painters.

the island from pirates, hence the intimidating cannon outside the entrance. The building is now used for community-based cultural events and exhibitions. There's a stunning view embracing the Playa Jardín. *Tue–Sat 11am–1pm and 5pm–8pm | Admission free | Paseo de Luís Lavaggi s/n*

ERMITA DE SAN TELMO

The small white chapel of San Telmo is situated at the southwestern end of the Lido overlooking the ocean. Seafarers built it in 1780 and dedicated it to their patron saint. After suffering repeated

Canarian church architecture – Iglesia
de Nuestra Señora de la Peña de Francia

damage it was completely restored several years ago. *Paseo San Telmo s/n*

IGLESIA DE NUESTRA SEÑORA DE LA PEÑA DE FRANCIA

Situated on the elevated Plaza de la Iglesia is Puerto's main church. Work started on it in 1684 and it was completed in 1697, however the grey, neoclassical bell tower was added only 100 years ago. The heavily-gilded altarpiece on the Baroque main altar, which dates from the 18th century, and several statues of saints, including the Virgen del Rosario and the Virgen de los Dolores create a remarkable spectacle. *Calle Quintana s/n*

IGLESIA DE SAN FRANCISCO

Built between 1599 and 1608, the church of San Francisco is probably the oldest building in Puerto de la Cruz. There used to be a Franciscan monastery next door, but now it is the *Parque de San Francisco* with music venue. *Calle San Juan/Calle Quintana*

JARDÍN BOTÁNICO ★ ●

In 1790 King Carlos III of Spain established the Botanical Garden to help exotic plants from the tropics to adjust to the temperate climate of Europe. Thriving on area of almost 2.5 hectares (6 acres) are cinnamon trees, so-called sausage trees, strangler figs, pepper and tulip trees, coral and breadfruit trees, coffee and cocoa bushes, araucaria, various fruits and lots more. The second stage of this ambitious plan, i.e. to acclimatise the exotic plants on the Spanish mainland, did not succeed. Plants that flourished in tropical climates did not like the cool winters of Madrid. But the Botanical Garden has retained its importance and has evolved into an enchanted forest of unusual plants. The most impressive plant in the gardens is a huge Australian gum tree. *Daily 9am–6pm | Admission 3 euros | Calle Retama 2*

MUSEO ARQUEOLÓGICO MUNICIPAL

On the west side of the Plaza del Charco stands the town's Archaeological Museum. Interesting exhibits here include Canarian ceramics, Guanche mummies, weapons and historical maps. *Tue–Sat 10am–1pm and 5pm–9pm, Sun 10am–1pm | Admission 1 euro (Thu free) | Calle del Lomo 9a*

PARQUE TAORO ☼ ●

The first grand hotel and casino for British spa guests was built at the end of the 19th century – with architectural features straight out of the Indian Raj – in a commanding position on a plateau overlooking the sea and the town. Former guests have included Winston Churchill and Agatha Christie. The surrounding parkland covering approx. 10 hectares (25 acres) has many attractions: as well as footpaths, there are lookouts, waterfalls, fountains, a children's playground and a restaurant. Within the grounds behind the former Hotel Taoro is a beautiful, terraced garden. Known as the *Risco Bello,* it boasts a fine array of beautiful flowers, plump fruit, an ivy-covered grotto and a water garden. *Admission free, water garden 4 euros | Altos de Taoro*

PLAZA DEL CHARCO

Puerto de la Cruz's main square, the rectangular *Plaza del Charco,* is the place where the locals like to gather for a chat in the shadows of the Canary palms and Indian laurel trees. There's a playground for the children. Of particular note is the *Rincón del Puerto,* a building in Canarian style dating from 1739 with wooden balconies and a luxuriously planted patio, now shared by two restaurants.

PUERTO PESQUERO

Opposite the Plaza del Charco is the narrow fishing harbour. When the boats ar-

rive back in port, buyers emerge amid a bustle of activity and the noisy haggling over the latest catch begins.

TORREÓN DE VENTOSO

This house in the Old Town, as slender as a church tower with striking yellow walls and contrasting grey volcanic stone, dates from the 18th century . It has been restored at great expense. It is said the tower was built so tall so that its owner, a merchant, could see ships arriving in port before anyone else. He could then be first on the scene when it docked and could cut the best deal! *Calle Valois, s/n*

FOOD & DRINK

INSIDER TIP ► EL CALABACÍN

A visit to this intimate restaurant near Lago Martiánez is an absolute must. The Harthan family have forged an outstanding combination of creative cuisine, fine

The most spectacular tree in the Jardin Botánico is this strangler fig

ingredients and great service. *Mon, Tue closed | Calle Uruguay 7 | tel. 9 22 37 09 38 | www.calabacin-teneriffa.com | Moderate*

CASA RÉGULO
Régulo, in a renovated town house, has become extremely popular. It has won several awards for its imaginative Canarian cuisine. Do try the octopus carpaccio *(carpaccio de pulpo). Closed Sun | Calle Perez Zamora 16 | tel. 9 22 38 45 06 | Expensive*

INSIDER TIP CITY CAFÉ
This pleasant cafe in the Columbus Plaza shopping centre has the best tarts and cakes in town. *Daily | Calle Quintana*

EL DUENDE ●
Jesús Gonzalez is Tenerife's star chef and at the same time el duende or the 'inspirational soul' in the kitchen. For him, it's not just taste that matters, but also colour and texture. The menu showcases several creative dishes, e.g. a variation of the tinerfeño favourite, *costillas con papas* (ribs with potatoes): At the bottom of a cocktail glass is the minced meat (no bones), on top sweetcorn, potato foam and a dab of coriander mojo. *Closed Mon, Tue | motorway exit 38, then follow signs to La Vera (TF-320) | La Higuerita 41 | tel. 9 22 37 45 17 | Expensive*

LA PAPAYA
Typical island cuisine served in an old town house with a lovely, leafy patio. One major plus point: a large selection of children's dishes. *Closed Wed | Calle del Lomo 10 | tel. 9 22 38 28 11 | Moderate*

SHOPPING

CALLE QUINTANA
You'll find everything – from art gallery to supermarket – in the pedestrian zone

in the heart of the Old Town. Take a look round the *Columbus Plaza* shopping centre with its attractive patio – many good shops selling everything from the latest fashions to cigars.

CC MARTIÁNEZ
Good, modern shopping centre also with a large selection of fashion stores, shoes, cosmetics and jewellery. *Calle Aguilar y Quesada*

MERCADO MUNICIPAL
The concrete market hall is not a pretty sight. But it's a lively place during the day as shoppers crowd around stalls selling fruit, vegetables, cheese, fish and much more. Also a flea market on Saturday. *Mon–Sat 8am–6pm | Calle Blas Pérez González s/n*

BEACHES

INSIDER TIP PLAYA DE BOLLULLO
Hidden away beneath a range of steep cliffs not far to the east of Puerto de la Cruz lies this 200-m long, pitch-black beach. There is also a small beach bar.

The bars and restaurants around the Plaza del Charco are popular meeting-places at all times of day

PLAYA DE MARTIÁNEZ ☼

The almost untouched town beach (250m in length) to the east of Puerto de la Cruz is composed of coarse, black sand with outcrops of volcanic rock. A boardwalk has been laid for walkers. Plus there's an incredible view along the north coast.

PLAYA JARDÍN

Huge quantities of dark sand were required to create this 'garden beach' to the west beach of Puerto de la Cruz. To ensure that all the sand does not get swept away, tons of rocks were dumped in the sea to create an artificial offshore reef. Good showers and toilets provided.

SPORT & LEISURE

The 9-hole *Golf La Rosaleda*, surrounded by banana plantations, overlooks the Valle de la Orotava, Mount Teide and the sea. Own golf school. Green fees: 1 round 18 euros, 2 rounds 24 euros. *Directions: Carretera Puerto de la Cruz–Santa Úrsula, km 1 on the left | tel. 9 22 37 30 00 | www. clubdegolflarosaleda.es*

If you prefer to get around Puerto de la Cruz by bicycle, you can hire mountain bikes from 54 euros for 3 days at *MTB Active (opposite the bus station) | Mazaroco Calle 26 | tel. 9 22 37 60 81 | www. mtb-active.com*

ENTERTAINMENT

Puerto de la Cruz has something for holidaymakers of all ages. The *Plaza del Charco* is a popular spot, with bars, cafés and ice cream parlours. The *Dinámico (daily)* on the square is an open-sided pavilion with a large bar, lots of tables and a good selection of drinks and snacks. At the weekend there's live music in the tiny *Taberna del Pescador (Calle Puerto Viejo 8 | daily from 10pm)* just around the corner from Plaza del Charco. Latin American and Canarian songs with guitar accompaniment. *La Tasquita (daily)* by the harbour is the town's busiest beer garden. Night owls will inevitably find themselves heading towards *Lago de Martiánez. Café de Paris* next door with a large terrace serves cocktails until midnight. Only after midnight and at weekends do things get lively in the town's 'entertainment quarter'. Canarios from the outlying towns and villages flock into the town to the chic bars where fine bands play hot Latin sounds. By 3am on a Saturday night, some parts of the town will be busier than in daylight hours as revellers move on from the late bars to the club scene around *Calle La Hoya* and *Avenida Familia Bethencourt y Molina*.

For a more sedate form of relaxation, above Puerto de la Cruz is *Abaco*, a superbly-restored country estate, which you can also visit during the day *(Tue–Sun 10am–1.30pm Canarian folklore shows | Admission 6 euros).* **INSIDER TIP** In the evening you can enjoy exotic cocktails at the bar, convivial seating areas in the rooms or wicker chairs in the romantic gardens. Concerts with jazz or classical performed by small ensembles regularly take place in the evening *(Thu–Sat from 9pm, Sun from 3.30pm | Urb. El Durazno | Calle Casa Grande | tel. 9 22 37 48 11 | www.abacotenerife.com).*

If your holiday cash is running out, then you can always take a chance at the *casino*. It is situated in the pool area by Lago de Martiánez. *Mon–Wed and Fri 8pm–4am, Sun and Thu 8pm–3am | Admission 3 euros (remember your passport) | Parque Taoro | tel. 9 22 38 05 50*

A pool under the palm trees – luxury and nostalgia go hand-in-hand in the Hotel Botánico

WHERE TO STAY

LAS AGUILAS ☼
This fully-renovated aparthotel perched high above the town boasts splendid all-round views. Idyllic location and very quiet. Some 219 suite-like units. Mini-club with pool and playground. Beach a short distance away, but shuttle-bus available. *Calle Doctor Barajas 19 | tel. 9 22 37 28 06 | www.hotellasaguilas.com | Moderate*

BAHÍA PRÍNCIPE SAN FELIPE ☼
Another fully-renovated, all-inclusive hotel with a fine location on the seafront with view of the Orotava Valley and Mount Teide. **INSIDER TIP** Get in early and book the corner double rooms with panoramic terrace. Several pools, spa, fitness suite. Good à la carte restaurants. *261 rooms | Avenida Colón 22 | tel. 9 22 38 33 11 | www.bahia-principe.com | Moderate–Expensive*

BOTÁNICO
This is one of the most prestigious hotels in Tenerife with its own gardens, lakes and sub-tropical feel. Grandiose architectural style and lots of marble may be a little anachronistic, but the 250 large, luxuriously-appointed rooms and exquisite service really are top-class. Terraces, pools, lawns. Guests can use the facilities of the exclusive *Oriental Spa Garden* free of charge. *Calle Richard J. Yeoward 1 | tel. 9 22 38 14 00 | www.hotelbotanico.com | Expensive*

MONOPOL
The beautiful, 250-year-old hotel in Canarian style is situated in the heart of Old Town and boasts a patio with arcades and new annexe. *92 rooms,* **INSIDER TIP** *when booking if possible request one of the 35 rooms in the old block | Calle Quintana 15 | tel. 9 22 38 46 11 | www.monopoltf.com | Budget–Moderate*

TIGAIGA TENERIFE ☼
Smart mid-range hotel with 83 rooms (ask for west-facing room if you want a view of Mount Teide). In a tranquil setting in Taoro Park with terraced garden, pool and a gorgeous view of sea and mountains. *Parque Taoro | tel. 9 22 38 35 00 | www.tigaiga.com | Moderate–Expensive*

INFORMATION

OFICINA DE TURISMO
Casa de Aduana/Calle Las Lonjas s/n | tel. 9 22 38 60 00 | www.teneriffanord.com

WHERE TO GO

LOS REALEJOS (134 A–B2) (*Ø G5*)
Situated some 5km (3 miles) west of Puerto de la Cruz is the municipality of Los Realejos (pop. 36,000), an amalgamation of a number of smaller settlements. It is worth a mention because the Puerto de la Cruz hospitality industry is now expanding into Los Realejos.

El Patio de Tita is a small colonial-style hotel in a banana plantation. The excellent facilities in the six apartments and their location in romantic seclusion are something special *(Calle Jardín 13 | La Zamora Baja | tel. 9 22 34 60 19 | www.fincaelpatio.com | Budget–Moderate)*.

El Monasterio occupies the premises of a former monastery. Small animals roam freely in the grounds, which are beautifully landscaped with plenty of greenery. Guests can choose between good, typical Canarian cuisine in the superb restaurant (excellent barbecue dishes) or light snacks in the cafeteria *(daily | La Vera | Calle La Montaña s/n | tel. 9 22 34 07 07 | Budget–Moderate)*.

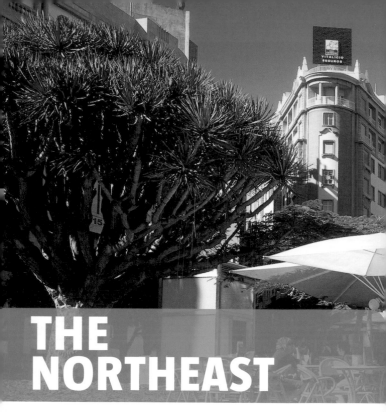

THE
NORTHEAST

The Cumbre Dorsal mountains separate both coasts like a backbone, climbing steadily towards Mount Teide in the southwest; at the other end in the northeast there are the largely inaccessible Montañas de Anaga. Only two winding roads lead up into this 1,000-m high range.

Tenerife's more recent history started in the northeast. This is where the Spanish came ashore and fought with the Guanches. They suffered defeats and celebrated important victories, which shaped the island's fortunes later on. The development of the island was also influenced by its geography, which could only support limited habitation. Farming families still live in narrow gorges and hidden coves, leading lives which follow an almost medieval pattern based around

work in the fields and the extended family. That is what life is like in villages just beyond the suburbs of the capital, Santa Cruz de Tenerife, a bustling metropolis where liberal Mediterranean values prevail. At the flattest point of the Cumbre Dorsal lies La Laguna, where in colonial times the leading figures in the church and the state resided. Since Unesco awarded it World Heritage Site status, there has been considerable investment, and the city is now finer than ever.

Settlements along the fertile northwest coast spread from La Laguna. Tenerife's 'grain store' is also the largest vine-growing region in the Canaries. And the region grows much more than that – everything from fruit and potatoes to flowers. Unfortunately, the impact of tourism is

Photo: Santa Cruz de Tenerife

A busy city and wooded uplands – from metropolitan Santa Cruz it's just a short hop to the almost deserted Anaga Mountains

often overlooked. Large areas of this often rugged, picturesque coast have fallen victim to an unbridled building boom.

BAJAMAR & PUNTA DEL HIDALGO

(130 B1–2) (*L–M 1–2*) Bajamar and Punta del Hidalgo are popular, usu-

ally quiet resorts much-loved by day-trippers from La Laguna. Built high but at low cost during the 1960s, the two places are currently undergoing a modest facelift.

The promenade and two large, free ● swimming pools, where salt water is circulated straight from the sea, are already complete. For people who generally shun tourists, both places, which are very quiet in the winter, make a good holiday alternative.

The Catedral Santa Iglesia in La Laguna

FOOD & DRINK

BAR-RESTAURANTE DORIS 🌿
In this simple restaurant with a large dining area, the menu is Canarian fish and calamari, accompanied by a great sea view. *Closed Tue | On the outskirts of Punta del Hidalgo on the left | tel. 9 22 15 66 16 | Budget*

ACCOMMODATION

INSIDER TIP **FINCA PICACHO**
Three delightfully furnished apartments in an old finca; in a great location, the complex includes swimming pool, gardens and footpaths. *3km (2 miles) southwest of Bajamar in Tejina | Booking by phone through Attur 902 21 55 82 | www.ecoturismocanarias.com | Moderate*

INSIDER TIP **HOTEL OCÉANO** 🌿
This boxy family hotel with pool and garden is situated in a tranquil spot. It has 70 bright, comfortable rooms and eight apartments with kitchenettes, all with balcony and sea view. Health spa offering massages, health and beauty. In-room massages available. *Punta del Hidalgo | tel. 9 22 15 60 00 | www.oceano. de | Moderate*

WHERE TO GO

CHINAMADA (130 C2) *(fl/ M1–2)*
The TF-13 coast road peters out in Punta del Hidalgo. At the end there's an 🌿 impressive view over the north coast and the Roque de los Dos Hermanos, the Rock of the Two Brothers. Starting below the bend is a waymarked **INSIDER TIP** walking trail (10km/7 miles, about 3 hours) to Chinamada, a pretty village noted for its cave dwellings, which are actually rather comfortable. Carved out of the tufa rock, the houses have attractive whitewashed facades.

LA LAGUNA

(130 B3) *(fl/ M3)* **Even the Guanches preferred the cooler uplands to the coast.**

> **CITY** **WHERE TO START?**
> Whether you arrive by car, bus or tram, your first stop really ought to be the city's historic centre. The best place to start an exploratory tour of the city is the **Plaza del Adelantado**. This is where you will find the tourist information office and you can buy an 'all-in-one' ticket for many attractions here.

This is where they maintained their summer residence. No wonder then that the Spanish conquerors also chose to build a settlement here in La Laguna in 1496. It became Tenerife's first capital.

It wasn't long before the town had become the archipelago's intellectual centre. In 1701 the first university in the Canary Islands was founded here. Although in 1723 it lost political power to the emerging town of Santa Cruz, with its university and episcopal seat La Laguna remains the cultural heart of Tenerife and it continues to be a vibrant city of 135,000 inhabitants. Its colonial legacy is still evident and nurtured, as is reflected in the many fine buildings in Canarian style, some of which are situated around the *Plaza del Adelantado* in the city centre. With its grid formation core, La Laguna richly deserves its Unesco World Heritage Site status.

SIGHTSEEING

CATEDRAL SANTA IGLESIA

A church occupied this spot in 1511. But most of today's huge church dates from the 20th century. The neoclassical facade was added in 1813, everything else has been rebuilt. A number historic works of art inside have been preserved, notably carvings by the multi-talented José Luján Pérez. *Plaza Fray Albino*

IGLESIA DE NUESTRA SEÑORA DE LA CONCEPCIÓN ⊹

It's worth a look inside La Laguna's oldest church (1496) for the painted wooden ceiling, a magnificently carved Baroque pulpit and a baptismal font that the Spanish conqueror Alonso Fernández de Lugo brought here from Seville. Next to the church stands a seven-storey bell tower from 1697. A viewing terrace at the top affords a fine view over the town and the

green uplands beyond. *Open at irregular times | Calle del Obispo Rey Redondo s/n*

INSIDER TIP ▶ MUSEO DE LA CIENCIA Y EL COSMOS ●

The Museum of Science and the Cosmos is visible from afar, mainly because of the conspicuous planetarium and huge radio telescope on top of the rust-red building. It is of interest to visitors of all ages, as it uses fun, interactive methods at over 70 different 'stations' to explain the mysteries of the universe. *Tue–Sun 9am–7pm | Admission 3 euros (museum), 1 euro (planetarium) | Calle Vía Láctea s/n | www.museosdetenerife.com*

MARCO POLO HIGHLIGHTS

★ **Cumbre Dorsal**
A panoramic tour along the 'backbone of tenerife' passes through a varied range of lands → p. 57

★ **Auditorio de Tenerife**
An architectural masterpiece became the symbol of the island → p. 60

★ **Iglesia de Nuestra Señora de la Concepción**
It's the architectural coherence that makes the church in Santa Cruz such a pleasing sight → p. 60

★ **Parque García Sanabria**
The large park in Santa Cruz is a welcome green space interspersed with an abundance of tropical plants → p. 61

★ **Playa de las Teresitas**
At weekends this gem of a beach attracts thousands of *tinerfeños* → p. 65

LA LAGUNA

MUSEO DE HISTORIA DE TENERIFE
As well as the treasures in the history museum – including a famous collection of maps – the building itself, the *Casa de Lercaro*, is of interest in its own right. Built in 1593, with its unique patio and richly carved wooden gallery, it is one of the finest examples of secular Canarian architecture *(Tue–Sun 9am–7pm | Admission 3 euros | 22 Calle San Agustín | www.museosdetenerife.com)*. In the *Fundación Cristino de Vera* a few doors further on you can admire the nearly 100 paintings by the Tenerife-born painter of the same name *(Admission free)*.

SALA ROSA MARIA ALONSO DE ARTE
This small gallery displays Canarian art up to the classical modernist era. *Mon–Fri 11am–1pm and 5pm–9pm, Sat 11am–1pm | Plaza de la Concepción 5 | Admission free*

FOOD & DRINK

ACAYMO
This cabin-style restaurant is situated 5km (3 miles) northwest of the city centre. At weekends in particular it is very popular with the locals, who love the fine Canarian cuisine. *Daily | Carretera TF-162 La Laguna–Tacoronte, opposite the Guamasa motorway exit | tel. 9 22 63 78 40 | Moderate*

LA MAQUILA
Renowned for its meat dishes such as *conejo en salmorejo* (rabbit in a spicy marinade), this restaurant is hidden away in a side street off Calle Herradores (between the two main churches). *Closed Tue | Callejon de Maquila s/n | tel. 9 22 25 70 20 | Moderate*

EL TIMPLE
From the outside and inside, this restaurant, named after a Canarian stringed instrument, looks like an old inn. But its proprietors are young and committed. Ana is in charge of the kitchen, while husband Benito alternates between kitchen and dining room. Most tinerfeños order a *ración* (portion) – and because it tastes so good, they can't resist a second one. *Closed Sun, Mon | Calle Candilas 4 | tel. 9 22 25 02 40 | Moderate*

SHOPPING

The traffic-calmed streets are lined with small shops and grocery stores. For good wines from Tenerife seek out *Viña Norte (Plaza de la Concepción, 16),* for handicrafts ranging from pottery and textiles to basketry, try *Atlántida* opposite the Episcopal Palace *(San Agustín 55 | www.atlantidaartesania.es)*.

SPORT & LEISURE

The oldest golf club in Tenerife is the *RCG Tenerife*. The 40-hectare (100-acre) 18-hole course is situated near the airport. Green fee: 75 euros, non-members must book in advance. *Access via the Autopista del Norte, Guamasa exit | tel. 9 22 63 66 07 | www.rcgt.es*

ENTERTAINMENT

There are many pubs and bars south of the *Plaza del Adelantado*.

BUHO
Musica en vivo several times a week in the 'Owl' club. *Daily from 6pm | Calle Catedral 3 | www.buhobar.com*

CAFÉ FOLIE
This pub revels in student-style velvet furnishings of the 1970s with ancient sofas and a faux hippie clientele. Retro at its best. *Daily | Calle Santo Domingo 10*

ACCOMMODATION

AGUERE

Located between the two main churches, this small hotel occupies a former church building. The 21 rooms are furnished in a simple, functional style, and there is a cosy, covered patio. *Calle La Carrera 55 |*

INSIDER TIP **NIVARIA**

Right on the *Plaza del Adelantado*, this aparthotel occupies a beautiful town house dating from the 18th century. The interior, with lots of wood, is a perfect example of Canarian style. *73 rooms and apartments | tel. 9 22 26 42 98 | www. hotelnivaria.com | Moderate*

There are good views of the Pico del Teide from the Cumbre Dorsal

tel. 9 22 25 94 90 | www.hotelaguere.es | Budget

CASA EL PORTE

Some 3km (2 miles) from La Laguna, in the tiny village of *Portezuelo,* Ana de Armas has transformed her ancestral home into cheerful, rustic-style accommodation with a large garden where orange and medlar trees flourish. The casa consists of two residential units for 3 or 4 people, each with its own terrace. *Tel. 0 40 5 60 44 88 | www.turismorural. de | Moderate*

WHERE TO GO

CUMBRE DORSAL ★
(134–135 B–F 1–4) (*∅ G–L 4–6*)

The 42-km (26-mile) journey along the narrow mountain ridge from La Laguna to Teide National Park is the best trip you could ever make in a car on Tenerife. Passing through a kaleidoscope of varied landscapes, the road climbs to a height of 2,300m (7,500ft). To the west of the old capital, cacti and orange trees bask on the arid plateau, at the centre of which is *La Esperanza*, a neat, if rather

Houses clinging to the hillside in the village of Taganana on the fringes of the Anaga Mountains

sleepy, village. Esperanza Forest begins higher up. Dense pine forests and tall eucalyptus keep the soil cool, ferns find shade, laurel and pine plantations will hopefully make up for centuries of felling. You will find it hard to resist the tasty home cooking, if you stop by at the rustic-style INSIDER TIP *Las Raices* restaurant in the heart of the forest *(closed Mon | Budget)*.

From the ◡ *Mirador Montaña Grande* at 1,120m (3,675ft), you can see La Palma, on the other side Gran Canaria. Entry into the cloud forest can often be abrupt. At the ◡ *Mirador de Ortuño*, Mount Teide, often snow-capped in winter, comes into view. In summer, the seven red watch-towers, one of which is visible on the left, are manned around the clock – forest fires are the biggest threat to this region. At 2,000m (6,600ft) the road reaches the tree line. The rocks are craggy, stocky pines, gorse bushes and low shrubs withstand the often harsh winds and wide temperature fluctuations. Jagged ridges of lava, along with black, leaden and red fields of ash, are evidence of volcanic eruptions that took place millions of years ago.

Shortly after the white towers of the *Observatory*, you will reach the National Park's *Information Centre* and the start of the lunar landscape surrounding Mount Teide.

MONTAÑAS DE ANAGA
(130–131 B–E2) (*L–P2*)

Northeast of Santa Cruz and La Laguna, roads that get increasingly tortuous wind into the cool Anaga Mountains. For millions of years the laurel forest has survived in this remote area, where there is still very little habitation. These steep inclines were out of reach even to the Spanish settlers, who from the outset indiscriminately felled the island's forests. In many places the woodland is interspersed with bizarre tree heath (Erica arborea) – large trees, from whose branches hang long strands of lichen. Like sponges they absorb the moisture from the trade wind clouds, which ascend in dense swathes. If the mist clears, the *miradores*, viewing points, afford great long-distance views. The sweeping view from the highest, ◡ *Pico del Inglés* (992m/3,255ft), takes in the Atlantic surf at Punta del Hidalgo and the beach at

Las Teresitas. At the Mirador Cruz del Carmen, an ancient farmers' track, the *Llano de los Loros,* winds for an hour or so through rugged mountain terrain. For a leaflet about it call in at the INSIDER TIP *visitor centre (daily 9.30am–4pm).*

The largest village is Taganana **(131 D2)** *(ꚍ N2)*, which lies in a broad valley beneath an impressive backdrop of tall mountain peaks. It is well worth taking a peep inside the triple-nave church of *Nuestra Señora de las Nieves*, which dates from 1506. The fine triptych in Flemish style is from the same period. There's a stunning panoramic view over the village from the ᎓᎓ *Mirador El Bailadero.* Here you will find the INSIDER TIP *Albergue Montes de Anaga y (9 rooms | tel. 9 22 82 20 56 | www. alberguestenerife.net | Budget)*, the ideal overnight stop for hikers and bikers.

SANTA CRUZ DE TENERIFE

 MAP INSIDE BACK COVER (130 C4) *(ꚍ M–N 3–4)* **Tenerife's capital rises back from the coast to-**

BOOKS & FILMS

▶ **Óscar** – el color del destino – international co-production by Lucás Fernández about the life of the Canarian painter, Óscar Domínguez, a contemporary and friend of Pablo Picasso. (English subtitles/2006).

▶ **The Clash of the Titans** – starring Liam Neeson and Ralph Fiennes, features the landscapes of Tenerife (2009) Other films shot on Tenerife include **One Million Years BC** starring Raquel Welch (1966), **The Land That Time Forgot** with Doug McClure (1975) and **Journey to the Centre of the Earth**, also with Doug McClure (1976).

▶ **The Deadliest Plane Crash** – in 1977 two fully loaded 747 jumbo jets collided at Los Rodeos airport killing 583 people – the full story (DVD/1997).

▶ **Tenerife: An English History** – a short history of Tenerife from volcanic wasteland to a destination for mass tourism (Kindle/2011).

▶ **More Ketchup Than Salsa: Confessions of a Tenerife Barman** – Joe Cawley, a British expat in business on Tenerife, takes a light-hearted look at life on the island (Kindle/2005).

SANTA CRUZ DE TENERIFE

CITY **WHERE TO START?**
The **bus station (Estación Central de Guaguas)** is situated south of the city centre. From here it's easy to reach the market (mercado) and the TEA Arts Centre in the Old Town. If you are arriving by car, then look for a car-park close to the **Plaza de España** and then start your city tour here.

wards the jagged mountains in a series of terraces; in the city sober apartment blocks and stately colonial buildings stand together in perfect harmony.

Although Santa Cruz (pop. 230,000) is a lively port, the pace is leisurely. Large parts of the city are either traffic calmed or pedestrian zones. Pavement bars and cafés are firmly in local hands, Canarian laissez-faire is the order of the day.

In 1494 the Spaniard Alonso Fernández de Lugo landed in the bay and established the first settlement here. Santa Cruz was initially overshadowed by La Laguna, 5km (3 mile) inland, but it has been the seat of Tenerife's government since 1723. Commercially important for the city is the sprawling port, where goods from all over the world are traded.

SIGHTSEEING

AUDITORIO DE TENERIFE ★

The snow-white concert hall is a daring building designed by Spain's star architect, Santiago Calatrava. Its most striking feature is the trio of huge, shell-shaped wings arcing over the auditoria, giving the building an airborne, almost weightless appearance. But not only is it visually impressive, the acoustics are also extraordinarily good. Every week

INSIDER TIP concerts in all musical genres, including opera and ballet, are held in the bright and airy halls. Tours of the building are also available (ask at the tourist information office for times). *Avenida de la Constitución, s/n | www.auditoriotenerife.com*

IGLESIA DE NUESTRA SEÑORA DE LA CONCEPCIÓN ★

The slender bell tower for the oldest church (1502) in Santa Cruz was built in typical colonial style and for many years served as an important landmark for sailors. After a fire in 1652, the triple-nave church with its many side chapels underwent several restorations during the 17th and 18th centuries. Slim volcanic stone columns support the building internally. Precious Baroque works of art include a high altar, a coloured marble pulpit, paintings, gold and silver treasures and the 'Holy Cross of the Conquest' dating from 1494. *Avenida Bravo Murillo s/n*

IGLESIA DE SAN FRANCISCO

This monastery church, beside the Museo de Bellas Artes, was built at the end of the 17th century. Of interest in the interior, which rests on volcanic pillars, are two altarpieces from the 17th and 18th centuries and the richly painted, carved wood ceilings. *Plaza San Francisco | information about concerts in the church available from the tourist information office*

MUSEO DE BELLAS ARTES

As well as 100,000 volumes belonging to the city library, the Museum of Fine Arts in the former Franciscan monastery contains mainly works by Canarian artists, but also paintings by Spanish, Dutch and Italian masters. *Tue–Fri 10am–8pm, Sat, Sun 10am–3pm | Admission free | Plaza del Principe Asturias*

MUSEO MILITAR DE ALMEYDA

This fortress dating from the 19th century is not just an administrative office for the military, it is also a museum. The main attraction being the *El Tigre* cannon. One shot from the Tiger during the 1797 siege

its flora and fauna and the history of the Guanches. Look for a collection of prehistoric skulls neatly lined up in glass cases. Tools, ornaments and everyday objects belonging to the early Canarian population complete the picture. *Tue–*

Nicely restored   Iglesia de Nuestra Señora de la Concepción in La Laguna

of Santa Cruz is said to have cost Admiral Horatio Nelson his right arm. *Tue–Sat 10am–2pm | Admission free | Calle San Isidro 1*

MUSEO DE LA NATURALEZA Y EL HOMBRE

The Natural History and Ethnology museum, which opened in 1997, later merged with the Archaeological Museum and is now accommodated in the restored former *Antiguo Hospital Civil,* the Civil Hospital. The building, now boasting a new interior with a bright and cheerful design, uses audio-visual aids and many other exhibits to chart the emergence of the island, the Canarian archipelago,

Sun 9am–7pm | Admission 3 euros | Calle Fuente Morales

PARQUE MUNICIPAL GARCÍA SANABRIA ★

This park south of the Rambla, named after one of the city's mayors, is unique throughout the whole archipelago. Numerous fountains, romantic arcades, huge trees and dense, subtropical vegetation attract locals and visitors alike. After a complete makeover, it now boasts wide paths, sculptures, idyllic squares, welcoming benches and a nice cafeteria. A stroll in the park is an essential part of any visit to Santa Cruz. A tourist train *(daily | 1 euro)* takes visitors on a full tour.

PLAZA DE LA CANDELARIA

This pedestrianised square opens on to the Plaza de España and forms the heart of Santa Cruz's shopping quarter. A striking feature in the centre of the square is the tall column topped by a figure in Car-

These tiled benches are really quite uncomfortable

rara marble, representing the *Virgen de la Candelaria*. She is Tenerife's patron saint.

PLAZA DE ESPAÑA

This newly renovated main square is dominated by the *Monumento de los Caídos*, a memorial to local people who fell in the war. Despite some modifications it is still rather harsh and unforgiving. Now it has been renovated, the broad plaza with its large circular wading pool, trees and floating droplet-shaped lights is a very attractive spot. In the background are two pavilions with roofs and walls

covered in greenery – they house the tourist information office and an Artenerife craft shop. On the other side of the square stands the *Cabildo Insular*, the seat of the island's government.

PLAZA DEL PRÍNCIPE ASTURIAS

A magnificent square named after the son of the Spanish king. Mature trees and lush vegetation create the impression of a sub-tropical oasis.

PLAZA DEL JULIO 25

Broad-crowned palm trees surround this small plaza. The fountain with eight water-spouting frogs and the 19 benches tiled with colourful mosaics have Moorish echoes.

LA RAMBLA

This long boulevard arcs around the centre of the city. Kiosks and benches shaded by tall trees line this pedestrian walkway – it's another place where friends and families gather for a relaxing stroll, particularly in the evening. Modern sculptures – including ones by Henry Moore and Joan Miró – bring art into everyday life. The old bull-ring halfway round is now only used for sporting events, children's festivals and pop concerts.

TEATRO GUIMERA

The theatre was renovated in 1991 and is named after Ángel Guimerá, a poet born in Santa Cruz in 1849; it was an important cultural centre during the 19th century. Today, it hosts concerts and theatre performances. *Plaza de la Madera | www.teatroguimera.es*

TENERIFE ESPACIO DE LAS ARTES ●

The TEA is the city's new cultural centre. Externally, this elongated complex fits perfectly into the barranco, the long ravine, which runs through the city towards the coast. Inside, strictly angled lines, tall glass facades and an open patio allow plenty of light in. High-quality permanent and temporary INSIDERTIP▶ exhibitions (admission 5 euros), a large library, cafeteria. Plus 36 internet terminals available free of charge. *Tue-Sun 10am–8pm | Admission free | Avenida de San Sebastián 10*

FOOD & DRINK

BODEGÓN EL PUNTERO
A town restaurant in the style of country inn – choose from all the Canarian classics. The fish served here is especially good. *Closed Sun. | Calle San Clemente 3 | tel. 9 22 28 22 14 | Budget*

EL COTO DE ANTONIO
This rather unassuming restaurant is situated near the Plaza de Toros and is recognised by the locals for its innovative cuisine. *Closed Sun evening. | Calle General Goded 13 | tel. 9 22 27 21 05 | Expensive*

INSIDERTIP▶ LA HIERBITA
Occupies an old house with several rooms in a narrow city centre lane. The young owners offer a large menu of typical Canarian dishes at lunch-time, mainly

tapas in the evening. *Closed Sun. | Calle Clavel 19 | tel. 9 22 24 46 17 | www.lahierbita.com | Budget–Moderate*

INSIDERTIP▶ KIOSKO PRÍNCIPE
This re-opened iron pavillon is a real gem – the choice of tapas is wide; the atmosphere under the tall trees cool and relaxed. *Daily | Plaza del Principe Asturias | tel. 9 22 24 74 40 | Budget*

LOS MENCEYES
Crystal chandeliers, upholstered chairs and elegant table presentations create a smart setting for international haute cuisine and new Canarian dishes. An army of waiters in tails stay calm and discreet even at busy times. One of the best restaurants on the island. *Daily | Calle Dr. Naveiras 38 | tel. 9 22 27 67 00 | Expensive*

SHOPPING

ARTENERIFE
On the Plaza de España stands a low, arcing pavilion covered in greenery belonging to the state art and craft chain. *Mon–Fri 10am–2pm und 5pm–8pm, Sat 10am–2pm | www.artenerife.com*

THE ENVIRONMENT IN A HOLIDAY PARADISE

Much of Tenerife's coastline is built-up and the waste storage depots are piled high with the rubbish discarded by the 900,000 inhabitants and the almost 3 million holidaymakers who visit every year. More and more new roads are being built for cars that pump out tonnes of CO_2 into the Atlantic air. Add to that the fumes from the oil refinery in Santa Cruz. But there are also some positives: arrays of wind turbines and solar panels are connected to the Institute for Renewable Energy. The visitor centre here is of interest, as are the '25 bioclimatic houses', which have been designed to make the most of the island's climate and are also self-sufficient in energy use *(ITER | Granadilla de Abona | www.iter.es)*.

EL CORTE INGLÉS ●

This large department store in *Avenida Tres de Mayo* offers shoppers everything – from the latest fashions and DVDs to fine foods. On the top floor, the seventh, there is a ☀ panoramic restaurant.

MERCADO DE NUESTRA SENORA DE ÁFRICA

It is an exhilarating experience to take a tour of Santa Cruz's produce market, which occupies a beige, Moorish-style building. In the wide square and beneath the arcades of the two-storey building, traders offer for sale animals, fruits, vegetables, fish, flowers, cheese and lots more *(daily 7am–3pm | Calle San Sebastián, s/n)*. On Sunday there's a flea market at the mercado.

ZARA

The now global Spanish fashion brand, renowned for affordable, but contemporary styles, has an outlet in the pedestrian zone. *Corner of Calle del Castillo/ Teobaldo Power*

ENTERTAINMENT

There are a lot of pubs and bars in the area around the *Plaza de la Paz*. Disco pubs and cocktail bars on the *Avenida de Anaga* promenade stay open until 4 in the morning.

INSIDER TIP ▶ PUENTE SERRADOR

A new scene is emerging in *La Noria* underneath the bridge. You can chill out in lounge style in *Arcos de la Noria*. Beyond that they come thick and fast: in *Lagar* there's live music, opposite the cool *Mojos y Mojitos* and *Los Reunidos* bars, then comes the *Marqués de la Noria* bodega and the classic tasca *El Porrón*. *Every day from 10pm | Calle Antonio Domínguez Alfonso*

EL SON

At the weekend the dancing in this Latino disco is to hot salsa and merengue rhythms. *Thu–Sun from 11pm | Avenida 3 de Mayo 75*

ACCOMMODATION

CONTEMPORANEO

The hotel's décor is modern and elegant, the rooms spacious and inviting. Sun loungers on the roof terrace. *150 rooms | Rambla del General Franco 116 | tel. 9 22 27 15 71 | www.hotelcontemporaneo. com | Moderate*

MENCEY ●

This archetypal grand hotel in traditional Canarian architectural style is situated in the city centre, on the edge of the city park and beside the Rambla. Fully renovated in 2011, the lobby and restaurant, lounges and bars evoke the spirit of a bygone age, but the rooms are thoroughly modern – unfussy and pure white. There is a palm garden with a pool and a large spa. *293 rooms | Avenida Dr. José Naveiras 38 | tel. 9 22 60 99 00 | www.ibero stargrandhotelmencey.com | Expensive*

TABURIENTE

This hotel by the Parque García Sanabria is delightful. Leather upholstery, sofa corners and contemporary lighting create a relaxing atmosphere, in fact it's the perfect place to while away an evening with friends. Rooms in minimalist style. *116 rooms | Avenida Dr. José Naveiras 24a | tel. 9 22 27 60 00 | www.hoteltaburiente. com | Budget–Moderate*

INFORMATION

OFICINA DE TURISMO
Plaza de España | tel. 9 22 23 95 92 | www. todotenerife.es

WHERE TO GO

GRAN CANARIA (O) (𝑚 O)
For a day trip to the neighbouring island (see also MARCO POLO Gran Canaria) take the Fred. Olsen Express catamaran from the harbour. This runs several times a day to Agaete and the crossing takes an hour *(return trip from 92 euros per person | car and 2 persons from 269 euros | tel. 9 02 10 01 07 | www.fredolsen.es).*

SAN ANDRÉS (131 E3) (𝑚 O3)
When the city fathers decided that Santa Cruz de Tenerife needed a beach, they looked closely at the fishing village of San Andrés 7km (4 miles) to the northeast. But the volcanic-grey pebble beach at the foot of a steep gorge was not attractive enough, so in 1970 they brought in a few shiploads of fine Saharan sand from what was then the Spanish colony of Western Sahara. This was how the seaside resort of San Andrés came into being. Gleaming brightly in golden yellow is the man-made kilometre-long beach at ★ *Playa de las Teresitas*, now much enhanced by clusters of palm trees. To prevent the golden sands from being washed away, a series of breakwaters were created at the two ends of the beach and parallel to it. During the week it is often very quiet. But on Saturday and Sunday, *cruzeños* flock here in their thousands. It's an attractive beach, but few tourists choose it.

There is a wide range of INSIDER TIP▸ small restaurants serving excellent seafood and fish in San Andrés. *Two restaurants with good reputations are El Rubi* and *Marisquería Ramón (both*

Sunbathing under palm trees and swimming behind a breakwater – Playa de las Teresitas

daily | Calle El Dique 19 and 23 | Moderate), both with a large dining room and pond, from which fresh fish are caught for the table.

TACORONTE

(129 E3) *(㎞ K3)* **As so often on Tenerife, the place is surrounded by bland new buildings; it is much more interesting on the other side of the main thoroughfare.**

For wine connoisseurs, it is definitely worth a visit, because Tacoronte (pop. 22,000) lies at the heart of the largest wine growing area on the Canary Islands. Extensive vineyards extend along the fertile hillsides. The dozens of *bodegas,* and even more *guachinches, i.e. improvised* roadside taverns, can be very tempting.

LOW BUDGET

▶ The *Casa del Vino* in El Sauzal offers wine tasting with expert guidance for only 1–1.50 euros per glass. *Tue–Sat 10.30am–9.30pm | Sun 11am–6pm | Admission free | www.tenerife.es/casa-vino*

▶ There is often no admission charge for exhibitions at the ● *Centro de Arte* La Recova gallery in Santa Cruz. *Plaza de la Madera | Mon–Sat 11am–1pm and 6pm–9pm*

▶ The *national museums* in La Laguna and Santa Cruz de Tenerife are free on Sunday

SIGHTSEEING

EL CRISTO DE LOS DOLORES
This life-sized statue of Jesus dating from the 17th century stands in the church of a former Augustinian monastery. The triple-naved church also contains a wealth of silver work, including the altar and tabernacle in the chancel; the monastery has a beautiful cloister. *Daily | Plaza del Cristo*

WHERE TO GO

LA MATANZA DE ACENTEJO
(129 D–E4) *(㎞ J–K4)*
The place name meaning the 'slaughter of Acentejo' recalls the momentous battle of 1494 between the Guanches and the Spanish conquerors. On that occasion the conquistadors suffered a humiliating defeat in the Barranco de Acentejo just south of Tacoronte in a fight against men armed only with Stone Age weapons.

SANTA ÚRSULA (129 D5) *(㎞ J4)*
With a population of 12,000 inhabitants, this town (12km/7 miles southwest of Tacoronte) is about one and a half times larger than La Matanza. Apart from a pretty plaza, Santa Ursula has little to offer. But beyond the coastal motorway lies the holiday resort of *La Quinta Park Suites* with several pools, a garden and sports facilities. *300 apartments | tel. 9 22 30 02 66 | www.spa-clublaquintapark. com | Moderate*

EL SAUZAL (129 E3–4) *(㎞ K3)*
In a picturesque location on a slope above the cliffs, Tacoronte's neighbouring town (pop. 8,000) can boast some fine examples of traditional Canarian architecture. El Sauzal is largely devoted to agriculture, particularly wine growing. It

Wine museum with tasting room, tapas bar and restaurant – Casa del Vino La Baranda

is also proud of its two venerable churches both dating from the 16th century: the *Iglesia de San Pedro* and the *Ermita de los Ángeles*.

The town's wine museum, *Casa del Vino La Baranda*, is now housed in an old 17th-century farmhouse. From here you can enjoy an exceptional view of the sea and of Mount Teide. Documenting the history of wine production on Tenerife, notable exhibits include a wooden wine press, barrels and tools, bottles of all vintages and lots more. *Tue–Sat 10.30am–9.30pm | Sun 11am–6pm | Admission free | www.tenerife.es/casa-vino* Dine out in the excellent ● **INSIDER TIP** *Restaurante Casa del Vino* with tapas bar and you will be served typical Canarian fare and excellent wines. Terrace with sea view. *Closed Mon | tel. 9 22 56 38 86 | Moderate*

VALLE DE GUERRA
(129 E–F 2) (*ΩΩ K–L2*)

Wine is produced, fruit and vegetables grown and flowers cultivated in the Valle de Guerra region north of Tacoronte. Just before you enter the town of the same name you will see on the left the *Museo de Antropología de Tenerife*. This anthropological museum, with exhibitions devoted to contemporary Canarian customs and traditions, occupies the grand *Casa de Carta*, an 18th-century farmhouse. *Tue–Sun 9am–7pm | Admission 3 euros | www.museosdetenerife.com*

LA VICTORIA DE ACENTEJO
(129 D4–5) (*ΩΩ J4*)

That the Spanish eventually subjugated the natives is recalled 2km further on in the name of La Matanza's neighbouring village. It means 'the victory of Acentejo'. Just over a year after the first defeat the men returned, but this time with shining armour and an even larger army. The aboriginal Canarians now had nothing with which to counter the superior force and were finally defeated. To give thanks to God's spiritual succour Captain Fernandez de Lugo ordered his men to start work on a church, which was fittingly named *Nuestra Senora de las Victorias* and it stands to this day.

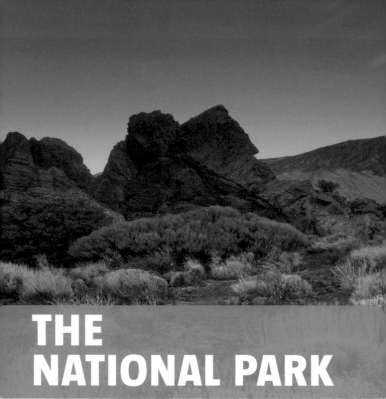

THE NATIONAL PARK

Established in 1954, the ☼ Parque Nacional del Teide (133 E–F 4–6, 134 A–C 3–6) *(ᗯ E–H 6–8)* **lies at altitudes above 2,000m (6,500ft) and covers an area of over 135 sq km (52 sq mlles). It is the largest park of its kind in the Canary Islands. The principal element is a giant** *caldera*, **i.e. a crater formed when the volcanic cone explodes, by the name of Las Cañadas.**

Las Cañadas (Spanish = ravines) is the geological term for the level sedimental layer at the foot of the caldera. At first it was assumed that there were two collapsed craters next to each other. The 3,000-m (10,000-ft) high volcanic chimney of the *Pico Viejo* on the northern edge of the two craters was created later on and it was here in 1798 that the last major eruption occurred. Recent studies suggest, however, that both the Cañadas and the La Orotava Valley were formed by landslides of almost unimaginable scale. At the time of the creation of Las Cañadas, a massive 1,000 cubic km (240 cubic miles) of land mass slid into the sea. It has been established that Mount Teide was formed around 200,000 years ago, after the landslides, and so in geological terms is still quite young. The area where the Cañadas are today was created by volcanic activity that took place some 7 million years ago, raising land out of the sea to form part of Tenerife.

The elliptical caldera of the Cañadas, with a diameter of 16km (10 miles), is one of the world's largest craters. Of its

Photo: Roques de García and Mount Teide

Aloof and majestic –
Mount Teide in the National Park
is an impressive spectacle

45-km (28-mile) long rim only the south-ern part has survived. Later eruptions buried the bulk of the north and filled the *caldera* with millions of tonnes of ash and lava. This is exactly what visitors to the National Park see today: a world of shimmering mounds of ash, plains, gorges and screes, sometimes smooth and polished, sometimes pock-marked and jagged; yellow and white with high proportions of pumice as in the *Montaña Blanca*; shining red and black through oxidation as at the *Montaña Mostaza;*

huge fields of cinders such as the *Luvas Negras*; tongue-like solidified magma flows; giant boulders seemingly flung by giants in the *Valle de las Piedras Arranca-das;* rocks, with jagged edges like black glass due to the high obsidian element, in the Montaña Ratjada.

Then there is the apparent lack of veg-etation. This impression is deceptive, however, as 139 species have adjusted to the extreme climatic conditions at high altitude. They have to contend with strong sunshine during the day, freezing temperatures at night and drought. A good 20 percent of plants are endemic, i.e. they only exist here. These include the pillared *tajinaste rojo* with its bright red flowers (Mount Teide bugloss), the little yellow or white Teide daisy and the Teide violet. Plants at this altitude stay in flower for only a short period, just May and June. Few vertebrates survive in these harsh conditions, with mouflon sheep returned to the wild, finches and kestrels being among the most interesting exceptions.

Most day visitors break their tour through the Parque Nacional in two places: The ● ☆ *Roques de García* (134 A6) (*ᗡ F8*), also called simply *Los Roques,* is an ensemble of multi-coloured rock outcrops. A viewing platform offers a spectacular view. If you climb a little higher, you will be rewarded with a stunning vista down into the *Llano de Ucanca*, the largest plain in the Teide-Cañadas and also of *Los Azulejos,* a shimmering rock formation in a greenish blue, due to the high iron hydrate content.

The second stop is the ☆ *Pico del Teide* (134 A4) (*ᗡ F7*) itself. Its almost symmetrical summit cone reaches a height of 3,718m (12,198ft). Its name is derived

from the Guanche word for hell. Emerging from its flanks come hot (up to 86°C) sulphurous vapours, proof that hell still stirs. The ★ *Teleférico,* the Mount Teide cable car, climbs 1,200m to La Rambleta mountain station at 3,550m (11,647ft) in 10 minutes *(open daily 9am–4pm in good weather | in May usually closed for maintenance | round trip 25 euros | www.teleferico-teide.com).* From there you can take walks to ☆ *La Fortaleza* lookout point and the ☆ *Pico Viejo* (3,135m/10,285ft) – but be warned: a strong wind often blows! Before or after your ride to the summit, you can sample the refreshments served in the panoramic cafeteria at the valley station.

If you wish to climb to the top of the volcano, you must obtain a **INSIDER TIP** special permit from the *Centro de Visitantes (La Orotava | Calle Domingo Hernandez Gonzalez/Urb. El Mayorazgo | tel. 9 22 35 60 00 | teide.maot@gobiernodecanarias. org | www.reservasparques nacionales.es | send or bring a copy of your passport).*

WALKS

★ ☆ *Hikers* can explore the Cañadas on a dozen or so routes, or even climb Mount Teide on foot. Scattered around the area you will come across countless *Huevos del Teide* or Teide's Eggs, huge boulders of lava rock ejected by the vol-

LOW BUDGET

▶ Guides from the *El Portillo Visitor Centre* in the National Park lead three free walks lasting between two and five hours. *Mon–Fri 9am–2pm | tel. 9 22 29 01 29 for bookings*

▶ *Mount Teide Observatory* organises free tours for individuals and groups, but by prior appointment only. *Tel. 9 22 60 52 00 | www.iac.es*

cano. Tours for independent walkers are well signposted (maps available in the visitor centre).

Please be aware, however, that high altitude puts the body under severe strain. Before undertaking longer walks, make sure you are fully acclimatised. Sun protection and plenty of water are essential for all hikes.

INFORMATION

CENTRO DE VISITANTES CAÑADA BLANCA (134 A5) *(ⓜ G8)*

Next to the parador is a visitor centre, where pictures, wall charts and multimedia displays provide background information on the National Park. *Daily 9am–4pm | Admission free*

CENTRO DE VISITANTES EL PORTILLO ● (134 B4) *(ⓜ G6)*

A visitor centre in a simulated lava tunnel with display panels, a multimedia interpretation of the National Park and an adjoining botanical garden where you can investigate Teide flora. *Daily 9am–4pm | at El Portillo at the north eastern exit of the Cañadas | Admission free*

WHERE TO GO

OBSERVATORIO DEL TEIDE ●
(134 C4) *(ⓜ H7–8)*

The strange white towers at the eastern entrance to Teide National Park belong to the Tenerife Observatory. When the Canarian Institute of Astrophysics started its work on this site in 1964, it seemed that here – well away from civilisation – was the ideal place to view the heavens. But today the lights from the holiday resorts interfere with the work of the astronomers, so they now observe the night sky from the neighbouring island of La Palma and scientists at the Obser-

A journey through the National Park is the highlight of a visit to Tenerife

vatory study the sun during the day. If you would like an (unguided) tour, you must register, ideally by completing the form on their website: *tel. 9 22 32 91 10 | www.iac.es*

> ★ **Teleférico**
> Spectacular – the cable-car ride to Spain's highest mountain → p. 70
>
> ★ **Walks**
> Incredible – fields of lava in the Cañadas → p. 70

MARCO POLO HIGHLIGHTS

THE SOUTHEAST

There are few hidden charms in this region. The land is arid and bleached by the sun, the plains have been randomly developed and unauthorised building goes on in the towns. And it can get very dusty – and gusty – with peripheral trade winds casting a milky veil over the sun.

The slopes of the Teide Massif look bleak and drab. Once this land was covered in dense pine forests. Later, the people set to work on the arduous task of terracing the fields, but cultivating them is hardly profitable – it is much easier these days to earn a living from tourism. Thanks to government subsidies, most of the retaining walls have been renewed. The region is doing better, because vines will grow here. If you have the time, it's worth taking the drive along the old, winding TF-28 highway from Los Cristianos to Santa Cruz de Tenerife. Not only are there many fine views en route, but the road is also lined by villages inhabited by people whose lifestyle has changed little since the arrival of mass tourism.

CANDELARIA

(135 F2–3) (*[] L5–6*) **Apart from the Virgen de Candelaria with its religious and historical significance, this small town (pop. 17,000) has little in the way of tourist attractions.**

But it is pleasant to take a stroll through the Old Town with its traffic-calmed,

Photo: Candelaria

At home with the locals – the south-east of Tenerife has so far remained largely untouched by tourism

sometimes rather steep, lanes and small shops.

SIGHTSEEING

BASÍLICA DE CANDELARIA

The triple-naved basilica built in 1959 in a rather fanciful Canarian/neo-colonial style is home to the archipelago's most revered shrine, the ★ *Virgen de Candelaria*. The extravagantly-clad Virgin adorned with crown and jewels occupies a place of honour in a gold-framed, il-luminated chamber above the altar. A recently installed mural tells the story behind the statue. Lost during a storm in 1826, a replacement was made in 1827 by the tinerfeño artist, Fernando Estévez. The skin colour of the Virgin and her crowned child is strikingly dark.

PLAZA DE PATRONA CANARIAS

The vast square in front of the cathedral was built for the throngs of pilgrims, who come every year in mid-August to pay homage to the Virgen de Candelaria. Highly visible on the waterfront are nine rather strange, larger-than-life *bronze statues*. They were created in 1993 by the Canarian artist, José Abad, and represent the *menceys*, who ruled over Tenerife at the time of the Spanish conquest. The Guanche kings are dressed in animal skins and are bearing spears, sticks and mallets, their clean-cut faces,

MERCADILLO

Three times a week a small market is held at the entrance to the pedestrian-only road, which leads to the Plaza Patrona de Canarias. At the weekend you will find a wide selection of crafts, knick-knacks and devotional objects on sale, on Wednes-

This faithful replica of Thor Heyerdahl's Ra II can be seen near the Pirámides de Güímar

athletic bodies and flowing hair seemingly idealising the European vision of the noble savage.

On the square, two traditional, terraced restaurants, *Plaza* and *Candelaria*, serve good, down-to-earth Canarian food *(daily | Moderate)*. After refreshment, you might feel like an exploratory tour of the town, but that could involve a steep climb. The small bell tower, which rises above the jumble of houses, is part of the Baroque *Iglesia de Santa Ana* (1575).

day farmers from the surrounding area come into Candelaria to sell their wares, mainly ☺ fruit, vegetables, cheese and wine. *Sat, Sun 9am–2pm crafts, Wed 5pm–9pm farmers' market.*

GÜÍMAR

(135 E3–4) (𝄢 K6) This lively town (pop. 16,000) lies in a broad valley, where in the past tomato plantations and potato fields provided the main source of income.

But most of these fields have been abandoned because of high water costs and a changed market. Now the townsfolk make a modest living from selling their wine. The bright green foliage of the vines stands out on the terraced fields. Before the Spanish arrived, Güimar was the capital of a Guanche kingdom. But their ruler, the *mencey*, quickly bowed to the supremacy of the Europeans and supported them in their conquests.

SIGHTSEEING

IGLESIA SAN PEDRO APÓSTOL

The church was built in 1610. In addition to the wooden ceilings and the carved pulpit dating from 1846, the circular retables (altarpieces) are particularly noteworthy, as is the illusionistic painting behind the altar, which appears to lengthen the nave. *Plaza San Pedro*

IGLESIA DE SANTO DOMINGO

The church was built in the 17th century to house the figure of the patron saint of the Canary Islands, the Virgin of Candelaria, and to protect it from the vagaries of the Atlantic Ocean. In the end, the move never took place. *Plaza del Ayuntamiento*

PIRÁMIDES DE GÜÍMAR ★

Spread over a large expanse of land to the north of the town are six stone ● pyramids. In earlier times, farmers dried their fruit and vegetables on the steps and gave no thought to their origins or strange architecture. Why should they? The whole of the island was crisscrossed by stone walls and every generation added new ones. It needed an outsider to take a closer look at these piles of rocks. Having studied the alignment of the pyramids and carried out a survey of their exact location, the Norwegian ethnographer Thor Heyerdahl concluded that they were probably used for sacred rituals and that they have astronomical orientations. He also believed they formed a transatlantic link between the ancient Egyptian pyramids and those of the Maya in America.

A *museum* vividly illustrates these theories and also sheds new light on the culture of the aboriginal inhabitants. Close to the museum is a replica of 'Ra II', the 12-m (40-ft) long ship Heyerdahl made from reeds. In 1970 he successfully crossed the Atlantic on the original vessel. *Daily 9.30am–6pm | Admission 10 euros | Calle Chacona s/n | www.piramidesdeguimar.net*

FOOD & DRINK

LA CUEVA ⭒

In a cave in the hamlet of Las Cuevecitas overlooking the sea. The fish dishes have a good reputation. *Closed Thu (irregular opening times, please call first) | tel. 9 22 50 69 02 | Moderate*

★ **Virgen de candelaria**
The canary island's most revered shrine: the dark-skinned madonna → p. 73

★ **Pirámides de güímar**
Mysterious stone → p. 75

★ **Vilaflor**
Famed for its spring water and as spain's highest municipality → p. 77

★ **Paisaje lunar**
A 'lunar landscape' of bizarre volcanic tuff → p. 77

MARCO POLO HIGHLIGHTS

ACCOMMODATION

INSIDER TIP CASONA SANTODOMINGO
This beautiful town house with patio, wine cellar, wooden ceilings and tiled floors dates from the 16th century. All six rooms have their own special charm. Very good restaurant serving no-nonsense food. *Calle Santo Domingo 32 | tel. 9 22 51 02 29 | www.casonasanto domingo.com | Budget*

HOTEL RURAL FINCA SALAMANCA
A small retreat in a dusty environment – an avocado finca in 5-hectare (12-acre) grounds. The property has 20 country-style rooms, plus a small pool. *Directions: Carretera Güímar–El Puertito, km 1.5 | tel. 9 22 51 45 30 | www.hotel-fincasalamanca. com | Moderate*

WHERE TO GO

ARAFO (135 E3) (Ø K6)
A gem in this village (pop. 5,000) 4km (2.5 miles) north of Güímar is the laurel-shaded plaza with a small bar *(daily | Budget)*. The 200-year-old country house,

known as ☆ *Cura Viejo* or 'Old Priest', on the outskirts of the village has three apartments and a sea view *(booking: Attur | tel. 9 02 21 55 82 | www.ecoturismo canarias.com | Budget)*.

ARICO (139 D–E2) (Ø J9)
This small town (pop. 7,000), comprising several districts spread out along the main road, lies 29km (18 miles) south of Güímar. **INSIDER TIP** *Arico Nuevo* is protected, because of its status as a Site of Special Historical Architectural Interest. Lining both sides of the downhill by-road off the main highway are some beautifully preserved village houses and a quiet plaza with chapel, all neatly white-washed and with doors and window frames in classic Canarian green – something of a rarity for Tenerife. The elegant 18th-century *Iglesia de San Juan Bautista* overlooks the plaza in *Villa de Arico*. Worthy of note in this church is the main altar with the Virgen del Carmen dating from 1767.
INSIDER TIP Typical Canarian accommodation is available in the ☆ *Casa La Verita* and the ☆ *Casa Cha Carmen*, two country houses in the hills between Arico and Fasnia. Traditional architecture combines with modern comforts; the magnificent vista, barbecue area and vegetable garden are a bonus *(tel. 9 22 50 07 09 | www.lasombrera.com | Moderate)*.

PORÍS DE ABONA (139 F2) (Ø K9)
This fishing village (pop. 2,000) lies some 18km (11 miles) further south and boasts a winding harbour promenade, plus a beach right next to it, if you need to cool down. The ☆ Café del Mar *(Closed Mon, Tue | tel. 6 26 39 00 96 | Budget)*, is worth the detour for the view of the bay and the delicious tapas.

LOW BUDGET

▶ You can stay the night in a double room in the remote Casa Rural *La Hoyita* near Güímar for only 36 euros *(1 room | book via www.ecoturismo canarias.com)*.

▶ The price is right at *La Charcada* in Puertito de Güímar *(daily | tel. 9 22 52 89 54)* – a meal of fresh fish or seafood usually costs between 6 and 8 euros here – and what's more, a table by the fishing port comes free.

VILAFLOR ★ (138 B3) (*∭ F9*)

This village, with just under 3,000 inhabitants and situated some 60km (37 miles) southwest of Güímar, is probably the most perfect spot in the southern half of the island. With some pride Vilaflor describes itself as the highest municipality in Spain. Around the town, which stands at 1,400m (4,600ft) above sea level, are many hectares of terraced fields, where local farmers grow vines and vegetables. One small business bottles spring water under the brand names of 'Pinalito' and 'Fuente Alta'. There is also an outlet for what is now a rare craft – just like their great-grandmothers some of the women in the village still make *rosetas*, filigree
● lace rosettes, which are sewn on to blankets and shawls. You can find the lace on sale in the souvenir shops on the church square, where the women will happily demonstrate the extremely time-consuming art of lace making.

Daily life in Vilaflor is undemanding. Far away from the bustle of the holiday centres and the dusty coastline, here you can breathe in the fresh mountain air of the Mount Teide region. Built on the site of an older chapel dating from the mid-16th century, the single-nave *Iglesia de San Pedro Apóstol* dominates the town's central square.

You want a holiday in Tenerife, but you want to be well away from all the coach parties and the noisy nightlife, then the cosy *Hotel Rural el Sombrerito*, a simple country inn, is the place for you *(20 rooms | Calle Santa Catalina s/n | tel. 9 22 70 90 52 | www.hotelelsombrerito.es | Budget)*. Another gem is the four-star INSIDER TIP *Spa Villalba*, with pine garden, sun terrace, spa, gym and pool. It is popular with walkers, bikers and climbers *(22 rooms | Carretera San Roque | tel. 9 22 70 99 30 | www.hotelvillalba.com | Moderate)*. Perched high above the town

Outstanding – the immense Pino Gordo Canarian pine

is the ☀ *El Mirador* restaurant, boasting fantastic views down to the coast *(closed Fri | Camino San Roque 2 | tel. 9 22 70 91 35 | Moderate)*. Not so good on vistas, but very cosy and friendly all the same is the INSIDER TIP *Rincón del Roberto* in the town centre, which serves up proper country fare and dry local wines *(closed Tues | Avenida Hermano Pedro 27 | tel. 9 22 70 90 35 | Moderate)*.

Starting just above Vilaflor are stands of ● Canary Island pines. One famous example of the species, the *Pino Gordo*, reaches a height of 60m (almost 200ft). It's by the road that winds its way up to Mount Teide, passing some stunning ☀ viewpoints on its way. One curiosity is the ★ *Paisaje Lunar* (138 B2) (*∭ G8*), the 'lunar landscape', a bizarre volcanic formation unique to the Canaries. It is to be found 20km (12 miles) to the north-east of Vilaflor (turn right near the km 65 marker, walking time 2.5 hrs/9km (6 miles) each way.

THE SOUTHWEST

Some 3.5 million of the 4.9 million visitors who come to Tenerife every year make for the southwest. This is where the finest beaches are and it's also where sunshine is practically guaranteed. In the last 40 years, an infrastructure that perfectly meets the needs of mass tourism has emerged – hotels ranging from cheap and easily affordable to super luxury, shopping centres, restaurants to suit all tastes, entertainment around the clock, plus leisure activities from hang-gliding to scuba diving.

It is also the location for the largest and finest water park on the Canaries – Siam Park. There are also half a dozen good golf courses, plus a number of marinas, from where pleasure boats leave for tours along the coastline.

But the global financial crisis has brought the building boom to an end until further notice. The golf courses with their grandiose club houses, a huge convention centre, expressways and mega-hotels built on what was formerly barren wasteland prove how easy it once was to attract investment.

But this dramatic transformation has endangered the traditional lifestyle of the locals. Agriculture is now is of little importance, the fields have been abandoned. There are some vast banana plantations, but these are mainly further north between Guía de Isora and Puerto de Santiago and in the land behind Costa del Silencio. In the south, tourism has brought prosperity. The holiday centres are now providing work for many vil-

If you want beach, sunshine and action 24/7, the island's south coast is the place to be

lagers – it's not a change that everyone welcomes, but in this arid region there are few alternatives.

LOS CRISTIANOS

MAP ON PAGE 86
(136–137 C–D5) (*E11*)
In recent years, the oldest resort in the south has seen some huge changes.

Roads have been traffic-calmed, pedestrian zones created and the beach promenade smartened up. But not much else has changed – crowds of holidaymakers keep the souvenir shops, restaurants, bars, hotels and street traders busy.

The Paseo Maritimo promenade links the old and new part of town. Just beyond, the beach teems with sunbathers and swimmers, further out fishing boats ply in and out of the small harbour. Strollers almost unwittingly seem to end up in the old part of the town above the harbour, which with its narrow alleys and tiny courtyards serves as a reminder that the now bustling seaside resort was once a quiet village.

FOOD & DRINK

MESÓN CASTELLANO

In a rustic Castilian setting surrounded by hunting trophies, lots of wood and wrought-iron chandeliers, Señor Manuel

12 | tel. 9 22 79 62 77 | www.taberna delpuertoloscristianos.com | Moderate

SHOPPING

LA ALPIZPA

Canarian crafts produced by people with disabilities are on sale in this stall on *Playa de los Cristianos* promenade. *Mon–Sat 10am–1pm and 5pm–8.30pm*

Playa de los Cristianos – plenty of room to enjoy a bit of 70s-style love and peace

José serves excellent meat dishes, grills included, plus wine from the mainland. *Closed Tue | Calle Alfonso Domínguez 40 (El Camisón) | tel. 9 22 79 63 09 | www. mesoncastellano.com | Moderate*

PICCOLO PALADAR

As the Italian name suggests, it's all about antipasti, pasta Roman style and changing specials every day – on a terrace overlooking the sea. *Closed Tue | Avenida Habana 11 | tel. 9 22 79 67 88 | Moderate*

LA TABERNA DEL PUERTO

Excellent location on the promenade; traditional Basque cuisine tastes good. Fresh seafood, prepared with care and beautifully presented. The fish, stuffed with ham, prawns and cheese is delicious. *Daily | Calle Dulce María de Loinaz*

INSIDER TIP ▶ **LIBRERÍA BARBARA**

Bookshop with Spanish, English, German and French titles, plus maps and guidebooks. *Mon–Fri 10am–1pm and 5pm–7.30pm, Sat 10am–1pm | Calle Juan Pablo Abril 6*

MERCADO DE AGRICULTURA

Super-fresh produce on sale on this fruit and vegetable market, much of it cultivated locally. *Sat and Sun 8am–noon | Chafiras, just west of the airport: TF-1, exit 24*

BEACHES

PLAYA DE LOS CRISTIANOS

The main beach for the town is 1km in length and up to 100m wide. It starts right next to the fishing and ferry harbour, is suitable for children and has its own lifeguard station.

PLAYA DE LAS VISTAS

The beach connecting Los Cristianos with Playa de las Américas has fine, golden sand and is lined with kiosks selling refreshing drinks and ice-cream. It is 1.5km (1 mile) long and protected by breakwaters, so ideal for swimming. At this point the swell is slightly higher, the wind stronger.

SPORT & LEISURE

Here in the south there is hardly a sport you can't pursue: squash, mini-golf, trampolining, parachute jumping, hang-gliding, walking, biking, climbing, sailing, windsurfing, jet skiing, scuba diving, deep sea fishing and much more. To find out what exactly is on offer, take a walk along the beach, around the harbours and in the shopping malls – you will see for yourself what the various options are. Or go to one of the tourist offices and pick up a brochure.

BOAT TRIPS

The modern catamaran INSIDER TIP Lady Shelley is based in Los Cristianos. Every day the boat leaves on tours of the in shore waters and to observe pilot whales and dolphins. *3 trips of 2–5 hours | 22–53 euros | tel. 9 22 75 75 49 | www. ladyshelley.com*

CAMEL PARK

Dromedary rides, taking 20 or 50 minutes, start from *La Camella*, which is situated inland a short distance from Los Cristianos. *Daily 10am–5pm | rides from 10 euros per person | Location: TF-28 3.5km (2 miles) | Free shuttle bus from the south coast | tel. 9 22 72 11 21 | www. camelparktenerife.com*

GOLF

There are three golf-courses southeast of Los Cristianos: the *Amarilla Golf & Country Club* has 18 holes, a 9-hole pitch and putt course, plus riding stables, tennis courts and swimming pools, green fee: 1 round 80 euros. *Directions: Autopista del Sur, Los Abrigos exit, 3km/2 miles) | tel. 9 22 73 03 19 | www.amarillagolf.es Golf del Sur* is located further west, Extending over 85 hectares (210 acres) is a 27-hole golf course, plus golf academy. Handicap required; Green fee: 18 holes 85 euros. *Directions: Autopista del Sur, Los Abrigos exit, 4 km/2.5 miles) | tel. 9 22 73 81 70 | www.golfdelsur.es*

≥ *Golf Center Los Palos* is a small, flat 9-hole golf course with sea view, green fee: 2 x 9 holes 32.50 euros. *Directions: Autopista del Sur, Guaza exit, 1.5km/1 mile | tel. 9 22 16 90 80 | www. tenerifegolf.es*

★ **El Médano**
A mecca for windsurfing and a meeting place for young holiday-makers → p. 84

★ **Abama**
A golf resort with luxurious facilities and first-class restaurants → p. 93

★ **Los Gigantes**
Towering up behind the village – truly gigantic cliffs → p. 95

★ **Playa de la Arena**
An extraordinary sight – a beach with jet-black sand → p. 95

MARCO POLO HIGHLIGHTS

LOS CRISTIANOS

Small fishing boats moored alongside yachts in Los Cristianos harbour

ENTERTAINMENT

In the evening Los Cristianos quickly quietens down. There is some nightlife along the promenade, the *Paseo Marítimo*. It's a little bit livelier along *Avenida de Suecia*. There are a series of cocktail bars, including the *Agua de Coco*. And in the *San Telmo shopping centre* behind the Playa de las Vistas, there are a few pubs.

WHERE TO STAY

ARONA GRAN HOTEL

This mid-range hotel in 1970s style, ornate with lots of marble, brass and crystal, is situated at the eastern end of Playa de los Cristianos and is blessed with fine views over the resort. Luxuriant hanging gardens give the place a tropical feel. *391 rooms | Avenida de los Cristianos s/n | tel. 9 22 75 06 78 | www.springhoteles.com | Moderate*

INSIDERTIP▶ MAR Y SOL

This spa hotel offers wheelchair-accessible apartments fitted with natural, non-allergenic materials. The restaurant serves vegetarian meals and will prepare food for guests with special dietary requirements. Treatments available in the ❧ therapy and rehabilitation centre range from massages and acupuncture to a rose oil bath. Fine views out to sea. The pools (one with water at 32° C) have access aids and hydro massages. Free beach shuttle bus, emergency service, diving school for the disabled, sports hall, golf courses and lots more. *234 apartments | Avenida Amsterdam 8 | tel. 9 22 75 05 40 | www.marysol.org | Moderate*

PARADISE PARK

This aparthotel surrounds a patio with pool. Guests are generous in their praise of the rooms, the food and the service. 20 minutes to the beach. *280 rooms, 110 apartments | Urb. Oasis del Sur | tel. 9 22 75 72 27 | www.hotelparadisepark.com | Moderate*

REVERON PLAZA

This is a place where you will feel totally at ease – a four-star hotel centrally located opposite the church and only a few metres from the beach. Attractive breakfast restaurant with harbour view, rooftop terrace with pool and basement spa.

Friendly, casual atmosphere. *43 rooms | tel. 9 22 75 71 20 | www.hotelesreveron. com | Budget–Moderate*

INFORMATION

OFFICE DE TURISMO
Paseo Maritimo Playa de las Vistas | tel. 9 22 78 70 11 | www.arona.travel

WHERE TO GO

LOS ABRIGOS (138 C5) *(ω G12)*
The abiding image of the village (pop. 2,000) is one of rectangular residential blocks made of grey cement. It is situated 15km (9 miles) east of Los Cristianos. Only after you have entered the village and reached the harbour area will you discover why tourists from all over the south flock here every day. Lining the promenade are several restaurants. Most of them are small and fairly basic, but they serve simply prepared, excellent dishes of fish and shellfish, which go pretty well straight from fishing boat into sauté pan. ☀ The beautiful sea view from almost of all of the restaurants comes free of charge.
In the multi-award winning *Vista Mar (daily | tel. 9 22 17 01 84 | Moderate)*, you have to choose your fish at the counter. The best sea view is from the narrow terrace of the *Perlas del Mar (closed Mon | tel. 9 22 17 00 14 | Moderate)*. Opposite the resort near the golf courses is the new *Hotel Vincci Tenerife Golf*. It's a modern complex with sea view, spa and excellent facilities all at reasonable prices *(125 rooms | Golf del Sur | tel. 9 22 71 73 37 | www.vinccihoteles.com | Moderate)*.

COSTA DEL SILENCIO (137 D–E6) *(ω F12)*
This 12-km (7-mile) stretch of coast southeast of Los Cristianos at the southern tip of Tenerife is described as the 'Coast of Silence', a name which might once have been an accurate description, but now this part of the island is regularly overflown by planes arriving and departing from the nearby Reina Sofía airport. In the bleak, treeless hinterland, the constant trade winds buffet the endless rows of banana trees and the expanses of plastic sheeting protecting the fields of vegetable. Lining the promenade in the former fishing port of *Las Galletas* are a number of ice-cream parlours and several fish restaurants, such as the basic *Marina* and the rather smarter *Atlantida (both daily | Budget–Moderate)*.

LA GOMERA (0) *(ω 0)*
Several times a day the Fred. Olsen Express hydrofoil whisks passengers from

LOW BUDGET

▶ The cost of amusement parks, discos, the casino, etc. can quickly mount up in Los Cristianos and Playa de las Américas. But promotional leaflets that grant free admission or discounts are distributed in hotels and out on the streets.

▶ Prices are relative – for golfers a green fee of 32.50 euros at the *Los Palos Golf Centre* → **p. 81**, and for health and beauty fans 30 euros per day at the spa in the *Sheraton Hotel* → **p. 92** could almost be a free gift.

▶ The delicious and sumptuous three-course set menu in the *La Fortuna Nova* restaurant in Los Cristianos costs a modest 7.95 euros *(closed Sun | Avenida Menéndez del Valle s/n | tel. 9 22 79 51 92)*.

Los Cristianos harbour across to the neighbouring island of La Gomera (journey time approx. 40 minutes). It's an interesting destination for a day trip. Return journey from 66 euros per person. *If you want to take your car, then the fare is 200 euros for your vehicle and two persons | tel. 9 02 10 01 07 | www.fredolsen.es*

A cheaper alternative is the slightly slower ferry operated by the Armas shipping company *(www.navieraarmas.es)*.

EL MÉDANO ★ (139 D5) (*ⓜ H11*)

El Médano or The Dune lies 20km (12 miles) east of Los Cristianos and is Tenerife's longest beach. Just over 2km in length, the *Playa Médano*, which starts in the heart of the resort, boasts fine, golden sand. In the section below the promenade, the beach – ideal for children and non-swimmers – gets almost completely covered at high tide.

A volcanic rock, the *Montaña Roja,* towers above the beach. Behind the 'Red Mountain' towards Los Abrigos lies the coarse-sand beach of *Playa de la Tejita;* it's 1km in length and always very windy. Nudists have claimed the first part of it for themselves.

Despite its attractions for tourists, the village of El Médano (pop. 3,000) has remained largely immune from the tourist invasion and is still a rather sleepy spot. There are still more locals than tourists. On the broad *Plaza Príncipe de Asturias* young northern Europeans and Canarians take a break over a beer. A kiosk provides tourists with information *(tel. 9 22 17 60 02)*. In the *Playa Chica* bar *(daily | Calle Marcial Garcia 24 | Budget)*, waves lap up against the tables, while in the *Caballo Blanco (closed Fri | Paseo El Picacho 8 | Moderate)* you can sit on the sun terrace above the surf. The *Cabezo* surf shop keeps windsurfers supplied *(Calle La Graciosa)*.

The village can boast plenty of good places to stay: Located in the family-run hotel, *Playa Sur Tenerife (74 rooms | tel. 9 22 17 61 20 | www.hotel playasurtenerife.com | Moderate)* is the *Surf Center (tel. 22 17 66*

Playa Médano – first attempts at windsurfing against the backdrop of the Montaña Roja

88 9 | www.surfcenter.info), which hires out boards (60 euros/day, 195 euros per week) and gives tuition to advanced surfers (from 35 euros).

Hotel Médano, elderly, but now refreshed, is situated by the beach in the centre of the town and is very popular with young people *(91 rooms | tel. 9 22 17 70 00 | www.medano.es | Moderate)*.

North of El Médano lie the stony Playa del Cabezo and *Playa de la Jaquita* – both are surfing beaches used regularly as venues for international competitions. The village is also home to the *Las Arenas* hotel. It is a large, boxy structure, but after a complete overhaul it can now offer luxury facilities: sleek styling with maritime motifs, accommodation in suites (ask for sea view when booking), outdoor and indoor pool and also a thal asso spa *(155 rooms and suites | Avenida Europa 2 | tel. 9 22 17 98 30 | www.hotel arenasdel mar.com | Moderate)*.

PLAYA DE LAS AMÉRICAS

 MAP ON PAGE 86
(136 C4–5) *(ω E11)* **Seamlessly merging with Los Cristianos is the tourist citadel of Playa de las Américas, which further north becomes the Costa Adeje holiday village. It is not a town in its own right, but a collective term for a number of recently-developed areas.**

It is at its quietest and prettiest at the north and south ends (the Fañabé/Playa del Duque and Los Morritos urbanizaciónes). The best accommodation is also to be found here. Running along the whole of the coastal area is a promenade lined with shops and restaurants. Clustered together in the streets behind it are hotels, apartment complexes, shopping malls, discos

and restaurants catering for the needs of the different nationalities, mainly English, Dutch Scandinavian or German.

INSIDER TIP EL GOMERO

The Canarian answer to pizza and burger bars. A very simple restaurant serving a wide range of good Spanish-Canarian dishes – all at very affordable prices. Very popular and often full. *Closed Sun | Las Terrazas complex | tel. 9 22 75 07 13 | Budget*

EL MOLINO BLANCO

Rural charm radiates from this pleasant restaurant. Note the solid wooden beams and several small terraces. The cooking style is upmarket Canarian. Look for the old windmill in the front garden, hence the name. *Daily | San Eugenio Alto Avenida Austria 5 | tel. 9 22 79 62 82 | www.molino-blanco.com | Moderate*

LA RANA

A rather unassuming, but much-acclaimed restaurant, which serves specialities such as milk-fed lamb and stone-grilled beef. *Daily | Avenida Las Americas Parque Santiago IV | tel. 9 22 75 25 22 | Expensive*

SUGAR & SPICES

This fashionable, black and white themed restaurant serves mainly Italian classics. Popular choices include pappardelle with cep mushrooms, tortellini with spinach and 'Diana' perch, garnished with mussels and prawns. *Daily | Av. Rafael Puig Llavina (Village Club) | tel. 9 22 79 22 71 | Moderate*

Playa de las Américas is synonymous with conspicuous consumption. There

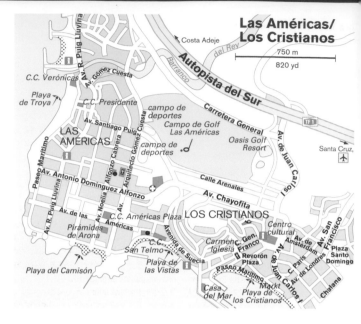

are plenty of malls *(centros comerciales)* with outlets selling everything from kitschy souvenirs to high-value jewellery.

ARTENERIFE

This state-run art and craft chain sells locally-sourced products. *Mon–Fri 10am–8.30pm, Sat 10am–1pm | Avenida del Litoral (opposite McDonald's)*. There's another Artenerife shop at the western end of Playa de las Vistas.

BEACHES

To the north, many small beaches have been created, all with fine, golden sand and protected from the surf by break-waters. So they are perfectly safe for children. The several beaches in close succession between *Playa de Troya* in the south as far as *Playa La Pinta* are very popular with holidaymakers stay-ing in the San Eugenio and Torviscas dis-

tricts. Hotels and apartment blocks are crammed together in a confined space here. The northern end of the conurba-tion is generally a lot quieter and there's plenty of space.

PLAYA DEL CAMISÓN

At the very southern tip and with a view over Los Cristianos is this gem of a beach – some 500m of golden sand with no traffic to negotiate and plenty of cafés to supply the sun worshippers with food and drink. Walk a bit further along the coastal promenade and you will come to a much-favoured spot – for a memorable sunset, sit and enjoy a sundowner in the ☼ ● beach bar of the *Villa Cortés ho-tel,* plus great view across to La Gomera *(daily | Budget–Moderate)*.

PLAYA DEL DUQUE

The northernmost is also the finest beach. No wonder it's called 'the duke's beach'. 600m of golden sand with jolly tents for changing cabins, overlooked by some spectacular hotels.

PLAYA DE FAÑABÉ

Some 800m in length and in a quiet spot, it's perfect for a relaxing afternoon sunbathing and swimming.

SPORT & LEISURE

Generally speaking, the sport and leisure facilities are very similar to those available in neighbouring Los Cristianos.

BOAT TRIPS AND DIVING EXCURSIONS

All the companies that offer these activities are located in *Puerto Colón* harbour. Two-hour catamaran trips with or without food on board on the *Bonadea* cost from 22 euros *(tel. 9 22 71 45 00)*, upwards of 37 euros for an excursion on the double-masted *Shogun (tel. 22 79 80 44 9)*. Royal Delfin organises daily boat tours to Los Gigantes and Masca *(50 euros | tel. 9 00 70 07 09 | www.*

tenerifedolphin.com). *Safari BOB Diving* is a company offering a variation on traditional scuba diving. Underwater scooters can be used by anyone *(48 euros | tel. 6 70 83 95 16 | www.bob-diving.com)*.

GOLF

The 18-hole *Golf Las Américas* course is located on 90 hectares (225 acres) of land near the resort. Green fee: 1 round 96 euros, online booking possible. *Directions: TF-1, exit 28 | tel. 9 22 75 20 05 | www.golf-tenerife.com*

The 27-hole *Costa Adeje Golf* blends perfectly with the environment. Green fee: An 18-hole circuit costs 87 euros. *Finca de los Olivos | Directions: TF-1 to Guía de Isora, exit to La Caleta | tel. 9 22 71 00 00 | www.golfcostaadeje.com*

The latest addition to the Tenerife golf offering is a ✦ 27-hole course overlooking the sea and La Gomera. It is laid out on a steepish slope to the rear of the *Abama Gran Hotel Resort,* a luxury complex with a park, conference centre and spa. With

You have to just eat fish here – all along the coast, there are restaurants right next to the sea

prices to match: 18 holes cost 200 euros. *Access via the TF-47, 9km/5 miles | tel. 9 22 12 60 00 | www.abamahotelresort.com*

THALASSOTHERAPY AND SPA

What makes the *Mare Nostrum Spa* in the Mare Nostrum Resort hotel complex so special is its sophisticated setting and many different physiotherapy, beauty and spa treatments. *Tel. 9 22 75 75 40 | www.marenostrumspa.es*

The **INSIDER TIP** *Aqua Club Termal* in Torviscas Alto is another great place for a pamper package. There's a wellness zone with hydro massages, Roman spa, seawater pool, sauna and much more. A 2.5-hour session costs a flat rate of 27 euros. Massages, lymph drainage and other special treatments are charged as extras. *Daily 9am–10pm | Calle Calicia | tel. 9 22 71 65 55 | www.aquaclubtermal.com*

From an atmosphere point of view, the ● *Thai Zen SPAce* in the Hotel El Mirador has to be the ultimate. Bathe in a minimalist-styled thalasso pool with water jets or a 25-sq m jacuzzi pool. Other features include fun showers, a hot-cold contrast pool and a hammam. Trained therapists run yoga sessions and give Ayurvedic and Thai massages using natural oils and essences from Asia. *Daily 9am–9pm | www. elmiradorgranhotel.com*

TRAIN

A white tourist train takes sightseers on a tour of Los Cristianos and Playa de las Américas. *Daily 10am–10pm | 9 euros | Departure: Corner of Avenida R. Puig Lluvina/Avenida Santiago Puig*

ENTERTAINMENT

When it gets dark, the neon lights come on. The crowds stroll along the promenade, sit in the shopping mall cafés or dine out in one of the many restaurants. Youngsters congregate in the *Veronicas* strip, the entertainment quarter along the main street near Playa de Troya, either in Tramps or in *El Faro Chill Art*. The

A grand arena – the Pirámide de Arona in the Mare Nostrum Resort

slightly older revellers (i.e. from age 20), on the other hand, gather in the cool music pub, the *Buda Bar (Avenida Antonio Dominguez, C.C. Arcade | Hotel Best Tenerife)* in the *Liquid Club (Hotel Conquistador)* or in the *Tibú Tenerife (Hotel Las Palmeras)*.

For a mainstream disco, there's the *Pirámide de Arona* (see below) at the Mare Nostrum Resort. For information about the current hang-outs for gays, consult *www.gaytenerife.net*.

Harley's (daily from 6pm | Calle Ernesto Sarti) aims to replicate the famous Hard Rock Café. Inside electric guitars, Cadillacs and juke-box music create the backdrop, while clubbers drink from a range of colourful cocktails.

Bright red leaves on a wild poinsettia

CASINO PLAYA DE LAS AMÉRICAS

If you enjoy a flutter, then the usual gambling games are available in the basement of the Hotel Gran Tinerfe. *Mon–Thu 8pm–3am, Fri–Sun 8pm–4pm | Avenida del Litoral s/n | tel. 9 22 79 37 12 | admission 3 euros (remember to bring your passport)*. Many hotels supply free admission vouchers.

PIRÁMIDE DE ARONA ●

Events staged in the auditorium of this imposing Las Vegas-style pyramid include **INSIDER TIP** ballet and flamenco evenings with the famous choreographer Carmen Mota. *Dates in the information kiosk in Avenida de las Américas, s/n | tel. 9 22 75 75 49*

WHERE TO STAY

ANTHELIA

This extensive complex was laid out in Italian Renaissance style. Characteristic features are a restrained elegance and first-rate fabrics in typical Mediterranean shades. Spacious garden and pool area.

A very quiet hotel above the Playa de Fañabé. *391 rooms | Calle Londres 15 | tel. 9 22 71 33 35 | www.iberostar.com | Expensive*

CLEOPATRA PALACE

A large complex designed in ancient Roman style, the hotel has the best spot on the quiet promenade, plus direct access to *Playa del Camisón*. 199 rooms and suites – but here's a useful tip: the rooms with **INSIDER TIP** even numbers have the best sea view on the south coast – with a marble bath and columned balcony. Large pool area. International restaurants serving excellent cuisine, plus entertainment every day. *Mare Nostrum Resort | tel. 9 22 75 75 00 | www.expogrupo.com | Moderate–Expensive*

JARDÍN TROPICAL

Opening out beyond the South Seas-style entrance is a world that looks to the east, to a mixture Arab and Andalusian influences. A snow-white building in Moorish style with soft, rounded forms.

PLAYA DE LAS AMÉRICAS

The tiled garden area is densely planted. Waterfalls gush over a grotto-like terrace. The 448 bright rooms are furnished with wicker and wooden furniture. Hotel and cuisine have won several awards. *Calle Gran Bretaña s/n San Eugenio | tel. 9 02 25 02 51 | www.jardin-tropical.com | Expensive*

INSIDER TIP▶ EL MIRADOR ⭐
The five-star palace hotel (adults only) stands on a low cliff above the ● Bahía del Duque, easily the finest beach in the south of the island. It offers suites with a four-poster bed and a spacious natural stone bath, sea views and large flower-festooned terraces. You will be pampered from morning to night with delicious buffets; magnificent pool area descending in terraces to the beach. Discreet, unobtrusive service and an almost intimate atmosphere. *120 rooms and suites | Avenida Bruselas s/n | tel. 9 22 71 68 68 | www.elmiradorgranhotel.com | Expensive*

PARQUE SANTIAGO III
The best in a chain of aparthotels in the south of Playa. The whitewashed residential units in Canarian style blend perfectly with the verdant gardens, pools and sunbathing lawns. Apartments and studios in different shapes and sizes. *255 apartments | Avenida de las Américas s/n, Los Morritos | tel. 9 22 74 61 03 | www.parquesantiago.com | Budget–Moderate*

PARQUE DEL SOL
An organised jumble of bungalows, designed in the style of a southern Spanish village. Benches and greenery alongside the shady paths. And the parrots create a tropical feel. *185 apartments | Playa de Fañabé | tel. 9 22 71 30 76 | www.parquedelsol.net | Moderate*

INFORMATION

OFICINA DE TURISMO
Centro Comercial City Center | tel. 9 22 79 76 68 | www.arona.travel

OFICINA MUNICIPAL DE TURISMO
tel. 9 22 75 06 33 | www.costa-adeje.es | Avenida del Litoral (next to the Artenerife shop)

WHERE TO GO

ADEJE (136 C3) (*M E10*)
This unspectacular but prosperous town on the western foothills of the Teide Massif is the region's administrative headquarters. At the beginning of the 16th century, the Spanish conquerors built the church of *Santa Úrsula*, with its beautifully carved coffered ceiling, here. Noble families did attend Mass, but sat in the gallery above the apse. The altarpiece for the main altar is a magnificent example of colonial Baroque *(Calle Grande s/n)*. There's a lot going on in the town, especially at the weekend ⏱ *Agromercado*, when farmers from the southern uplands come to the ● market hall to sell their produce. But it's not just fruit and vegetables they sell; the stalls are well stocked with honey, wine and liqueurs, cheese, cakes and aniseed bread *(Sat, Sun 8am–2pm | Calle Archajara, s/n)*.
At the upper end of *Calle de los Molinos* the ⭐ *Otelo* restaurant *(closed Tue | Budget–Moderate)* not only serves very acceptable Canarian fare at reasonable prices, it also boasts great views over Adeje. But this is also where one of the island's best-known walks starts: the ⭐ *Barranco del Infierno*. Because it attracts huge crowds, there is a limit to the number of daily visitors. Often the trail can be blocked by falling rocks. So if possible, it is advisable to call before

setting off. (Daily 8.30am–4pm | tel. 9 22 78 28 85 | Admission 3 euros (Sun free) | Walking time approx. 3 hours | Generally closed after rain | www.barrancodel infierno.es). A narrow path, formerly used by shepherds, winds its way up into the barren mountains. There is no shade, so make sure you have some form of head protection. Later on, as you approach the narrow, shaded 'Hell's Gorge' with its meandering stream, the vegetation becomes less sparse. When you reach the end of the gorge, you might be able to admire a waterfall that drops over 80m (260ft) – but only if there has been recent rain.

ARONA (137 D4) (*⌖ E–F10*)

Overshadowed by the huge Roque del Conde, it is hard to believe that this sleepy town is the administrative centre responsible for the two seemingly inexhaustible gold mines of Los Cristianos and Playa de Las Américas. Of the many billions of euros that tourism brings to

the region, very little of it is spent in Arona, but it still boasts an attractive town hall beside a square shaded by Indian laurels. Beside it stands a church dating from 1627.

For tourists wishing to spend more time in the town, then there are a few attractive hotels higher up, notably the ✪ *Ecohotel La Correa,* a rustic farmhouse on a green hillside run according to good environmental guidelines. Breakfast has to be 'organic', because Señora Luba runs a health food store. The room to choose, if you get the chance, would be one of the three suites in the annexe, which overlooks almond trees and the mountains (6 rooms | Camino de San Antonio 58 | tel. 9 22 72 57 38 | Moderate). Some 8km (5 miles) north of Arona is the *El Nogal* hotel, which occupies a country house dating from the 18th century. Since that time, it has been in the Linares family, who also run a good restaurant here. Old floorboards and beamed ceilings help to create an intimate atmosphere; there's

Wild Tenerife – it's all around you in the Barranco del Infierno

an indoor pool and a sauna *(39 rooms | Camino Real La Escalona | tel. 9 22 72 60 50 | www.hotelnogal.net | Moderate)*. Closer to town are the **INSIDER TIP** *Casas del Pintor.* A resident in one of the houses is the artist Carlo Forte, but another four are available to rent. All have a kitchen and a secluded garden terrace, where you can sit and help yourself to avocado pears, papayas, mangoes and apples. Between palm tree and dragon trees is a barbecue and there is also a small library. If requested, Carlo will give workshops on 'intuitive painting' and 'colorpuncture' *(Calle Mazapé 20 | Location: TF-51, turn off after 4.3 km (2.6 miles) towards Roque de Conde | tel. 9 22 72 52 74 | www.casaruraldelpintor.com | Moderate)*.

You can eat well in Arona too. The classic is *El Gomero:* for decades, the same grizzled waiters have been serving Canarian cuisine in this rustic setting at such reasonable prices that many locals also choose to dine here *(closed Sun | Ed. Las Terrazas 5 | tel. 9 22 75 07 13 | Budget–Moderate)*.

LA CALETA (136 C4) (*ω D10*)

The fishing village has morphed into a holiday resort. There are two leading hotels: on the edge of the village is the *Sheraton La Caleta (284 rooms | tel. 9 22 16 20 00 | www.sheratonlacaleta.com | Expensive)*, a rust-red complex in North African style. It can boast several pools in an extensive garden, and its own spa, including Ayurvedic therapies. The *Plantación del Sur*, also five stars, was built in the style of a Canarian finca. It is higher up – with stunning views of La Gomera – and in a very intimate atmosphere *(165 rooms | tel. 9 22 71 84 83 | www.vinccihoteles.com | Expensive)*. The four-star *H10 Costa Adeje Palace,* also on the beach promenade, can also offer luxury accommodation.

Holidaymakers with children will feel at ease here, as family rooms are very spacious. And if it rains, there's an indoor swimming pool *(467 rooms | Playa de la Enramada | tel. 9 22 71 41 71 | www.h10.es | Expensive)*.

Right by the water's edge is the ☆ **INSIDER TIP** *La Caleta* restaurant. The open balcony above the rocks is a great place to dine. A wide selection of tapas, meat and fish included on a long menu *(daily | tel. 9 22 78 06 75 | Moderate)*. If you don't fancy tapas, but prefer to eat oriental style, then it would be hard to beat the intimate *Kamakura, a* Japanese restaurant serving delicious sushi and tepanyaki dishes *(closed Mon, Tue | in the Sheraton Hotel | tel. 9 22 16 20 00 | Expensive)*.

PLAYA PARAÍSO
(136 B3) (*ω D10*)

Playa Paraiso has a small beach, a rocky bay for a dip in the sea and the *Lago Paraíso* pool area *(daily 10am–6pm | Admission 6 euros)*. The five-star *Roca Nivaria* hotel is an uncomplicated complex right by the sea with a good range

San Juan and Alcalá seem so out-of-the-way – and yet there are two five-star hotels here

of sport and leisure facilities *(298 rooms | Avenida Adeje 300 | tel. 9 22 74 02 02 | www.rocanivaria.com | Expensive)*.

SAN JUAN/PLAYA DE ALCALÁ
(136 A–B2) *(⊠ C9)*
Emerging like a mirage outside the resort of San Juan is the rust-red ★*Abama*, a huge luxury resort in Moroccan kasbah style. It has everything, even its own golf course. There are villa complexes at several levels running right down to the sea. A park, seven pools, a spa, nine restaurants – everything here is simply the best. *450 rooms and garden suites | Location: TF-47, 9 km/5 miles | tel. 9 22 12 60 00 | www.abamahotelresort.com | Expensive.* The Palacio de Isora resort hotel in Alcalá is the sort of place that sets benchmarks. This vast complex in southern Spanish style is situated by a rocky beach with views of La Gomera. Great seawater pool with jacuzzis, gardens, five restaurants and bistros, various bars, discos and luxurious designer rooms, plus a first-class spa. *609 rooms and suites | tel. 9 22 86 90 00 | www.gran-melia-palacio-de-isora. com/es | Expensive*

The resorts themselves can look rather dull and colourless from the main road, but it's worth making your way down to the harbour, which has managed to retain the charm of a bygone age. There is an artificial beach in San Juan. And work is in hand on one for Alcalá.

PUERTO DE SANTIAGO

(132 B–C5) *(⊠ C8)* **There is not much of interest to see in this former fishing village (pop. 2,000). New developments cover the coastal strip with its lead-grey cliffs.**
And yet, although this is the only place in the area with any history, it is still comparatively quiet. Around the harbour, which is reached via a steep, narrow street, the villagers live here very much as before. Women stand on their doorsteps and talk loudly to their neighbours. Men tinker with their wooden boats, which, framed by towering cliffs, bob up and down on the water beyond the 50-m wide beach of dark sand.

FOOD & DRINK

EL MESÓN

This Canarian restaurant is renowned not just for its good food, but also for its friendly service. *Closed Sun | Carretera General s/n | tel. 9 22 86 04 76 | Moderate*

LA TERRAZA

An uncomplicated restaurant with terrace, where you can eat decent pasta, pizza and fish while gazing out over boats at anchor. *Daily | Poblado Marinero 19 | tel. 9 22 86 70 24 | Moderate*

WHERE TO STAY

BARCELÓ SANTIAGO

The location of this vast complex on a cliff-top is particularly impressive. Directly opposite is the island of La Gomera. So, if possible, ask for a room with sea view. *406 rooms | Calle la Hondura 8 | tel. 9 22 86 09 12 | www.barcelo.com | Moderate*

COSTA LOS GIGANTES ☆

An all-inclusive resort on a cliff-top. 518 family-friendly, sea view suites with living room and bedroom, so ideal for two adults with children. For the children there's a games room, cinema, pool with water slide, mini-disco and a special buffet. *Calle Juan Manuel Capdevielle 8 | tel. 9 22 86 72 72 | www.costalosgigantes. com | Moderate*

TAMAIMO TROPICAL

Built in a circle around a beautifully landscaped garden with palm trees and a huge pool, this complex has no fewer than 372 apartments. *Calle la Hondura s/n | tel. 9 22 86 06 38 | www.hotelesglobales.com | Budget*

INFORMATION

OFICINA DE TURISMO

Centro Comercial Seguro el Sol Calle Manuel Ravelo 20 | tel. 9 22 86 03 48 | www. santiagodelteide.com

Drinking coffee against the colossal coastal backdrop of Los Gigantes

WHERE TO GO

LOS GIGANTES ⭐ (132 B5) (*ꟷ C8*)

Los Gigantes or 'The Giants' are a series of spectacular cliffs just north of the village of the same name. The cliff face drops 450m (1,500ft) vertically into the sea. Tucked beneath the rocks is the quiet village of Los Gigantes, at its heart a maze of narrow lanes, many of which are one-way. The view out to the cliffs is overwhelming, especially from the big pleasure marina, where many Atlantic yachts are moored. Los Gigantes are even more impressive, when viewed from a boat. The former shrimper 'Katrin', with owner Heiko Kuschnik at the helm, is just one of a number of boats that take sightseers out to the cliffs. They also run trips out to observe colonies of dolphins and whales *(daily from 11.30am | 2-hour trip 25 euros | 100m before the harbour entrance on the right | tel. 9 22 86 03 32)*. Hidden away behind the breakwater is the quiet INSIDER TIP Poblado Marinero, an apartment complex laid out like a Canarian village with a seawater pool *(93 apartments | Acantilados de los Gigantes | tel. 9 22 86 09 66 | www.elhotelito.com | Budget)*.

Beneath the 'giants' is the 200-m wide *Playa de los Guíos*, a beach of fine, dark sand, often closed due to rock falls. On the menu in *Miranda's* restaurant are a good range of local dishes. *Daily | Calle Flor de Pascua | tel. 9 22 86 02 07 | Moderate*. For more information about the village and the Playa de la Arena, log on to *www.losgigantes.com*

GUÍA DE ISORA (133 D6) (*ꟷ D8*)

Bananas, whole plantations of which surround the village, provide a livelihood for some of the 5,200 or so inhabitants of Guía de Isora, 10km (7 miles) southeast of Puerto de Santiago. If you have a penchant for unusual delicacies then make a short detour to *Chío*. In the wonderful INSIDER TIP 🙂 *Delicias del Sol* shop you can buy jams and chutneys made from ● exotic fruits, mojo sauces in every flavour, fig and walnut cakes, organic wines and liqueurs, as well as wholegrain breads and pastries *(daily, closed Fri, Sat in summer | on the main street in Chío | TF-82 32.5km/20 miles | www.delicias delsol.eu)*. Starting above Guías is one of three access roads to Teide National Park, ⤴ a magnificent car journey, first through farmland and then across a barren volcanic region at an altitude of 2,000m (6,500ft).

PLAYA DE LA ARENA ⭐

(126 B5) (*ꟷ C8*)

Originally designed to be a holiday resort in its own right, Playa de la Arena merged with Puerto de Santiago long ago. Playa de la Arena is the name for the resort's 250-m long beach noted for its fine, jet-black sand. Bright green palm trees by the shoreline create a splendid contrast. It is worth bearing in mind that this little resort has the highest level of solar radiation on the island. In recent years, Playa de la Arena has regularly been awarded the prestigious Blue Flag for the quality of its beach and seawater. The general facilities are also excellent: loungers (for hire), toilets, lifeguards, and the *Casa Pancho* restaurant on the beach has received numerous awards for its cuisine. Here's a tip for gourmets with big appetites: do try the excellent INSIDER TIP six course menu for 40 euros *(closed Mon | tel. 9 22 86 13 23 | Expensive)*. The *Playa La Arena* is the town's leading hotel. Remarkably, ⤴ all 432 rooms in the large, bright complex have a sea view. Good child supervision on the hotel's own playground. *Tel. 22 86 29 20 9 | www.springhoteles.com | Moderate*

TRIPS & TOURS

The tours are marked in green in the road atlas,
the pull-out map and on the back cover

① IN THE ANAGA LAUREL FOREST

The Anaga Mountains region in the far northeast of the island is almost virgin territory. Many of the steep wooded slopes are totally inaccessible. That's a good thing for the laurel forest. It has survived here; elsewhere it would have been wiped out. The evergreen trees absorb moisture from the trade winds and then water drips down the long, thin lichen braids that hang from the branches of trees, ensuring a vigorous undergrowth of moss and ferns. The area is sparsely populated. A few desperately poor hamlets have survived on various rocky outcrops, plus one or two fishing villages – and they can only be reached via interminable sequences of hairpin bends.

The tour starts in La Laguna → p. 54, easily accessible by motorway from the resorts in the north and the south. From here, take the TF-12 to Las Mercedes, where the laurel forest begins. It's worth making a stop at the ☀ Mirador de Jardina, from where you can survey over half the island as far as Mount Teide. Soon after you will reach the ☀ Mirador Cruz del Carmen, where a well-camouflaged ⏲ visitor centre will supply you with information about all the walking trails in the region. There is also a small chapel, a bar and a tiny market at the weekends. Another viewpoint, the ☀ Mirador Pico del Inglés, provides a different vista down over the northwest and northeast coasts.

Inland and upwards – discover the other side of Tenerife beyond beach and sea

You can keep deviating from the TF-12 to explore lonely hamlets, such as Las Carboneras, Chinamada, Taborno and Afur. But you may prefer to keep going until you reach a fork. The left turning is the TF-123, which peters out after **Chamorga**, but carry straight on as far as the picturesque coastal villages of Taganana, Roque de las Bodegas and Benijo (signposted San Andrés). The road (now the ⛵ TF-134) drops down to them in sweeping bends – worth the effort for the INSIDERTIP magnificent

views over sharply-defined ridges. Stop off for lunch in one of the fish restaurants in **Roque de las Bodegas** and, while you eat, enjoy a great view of the wild surf; in **Benijo** turn round and head back up to the TF-123.

From the spine of the Anaga Mountains it is now downhill once more, on the TF-12 again, to the east side of the island and the fishing and seaside resort of **San Andrés** → p. 65. You can have a bite to eat here or go for a swim on a fine beach. Now return to Santa Cruz. Follow signs to

La Laguna for the north coast or take the TF-1 motorway to the resorts in the south.

2 STEEP GORGES AND WINDY COASTLINES

If you are staying in the south of Tenerife, you should give yourself at least one day away from the sun and sea and explore the island's wild side. Rising up in the far northwest is the Teno Massif, an almost forgotten region of untamed mountains and jagged peaks. Time seems to have stood still in some of these tiny villages. Keep to the coast where the winds whistle round the Punta de Teno. After that, look forward to one magnificent little spot and then one of Tenerife's most striking landmarks. If you've got a head for heights and are prepared for bad weather – let's go! You must allow a full day, even though the tour itself is only about 100km (60 miles) long.

Starting from **Puerto de Santiago** → p. 93, it is just a stone's throw to what is a truly impressive spectacle, **Los Gigantes** → p. 95. The tops of these towering cliffs, the 'Giants', rise to 450m (1,500ft) above the village of the same name.

They dwarf houses, boats and people. Los Gigantes are at the southern end of the Teno Massif and foreshadow the inaccessible mountains further north.

The TF-454 climbs through countless hairpin bends on its way towards **Santiago del Teide** → p. 37, initially passing banana and tomato plantations. If you fancy some local pottery as a souvenir, then make a detour to **Arguayo** → p. 37. In order to continue a tradition that dates back centuries, an old workshop has been restored and visitors are welcome to watch the skilled potters at work and browse the small showroom.

In Santiago take the TF-436 to Masca. A breathtaking journey is about to begin.

A warm welcome – brightly-painted facades in the Old Town of La Laguna

The rugged **Macizo de Teno** – the Teno Mountains → p. 36 – is geologically a very old formation. Over the millennia erosion has gnawed away at the volcanic rock. Time seems to have stood still in these tiny villages, where the houses are built with natural stone. From the ◁◁ **Mirador de Cherfe** you get your first glimpse of hamlet of Masca, which until the 1980s managed without any road connection to the outside world. It balances on steep-sided rocky outcrop above the gorge, as if it is about to take off.

A tour through **Masca** → p. 36, a dispersed village, will involve treading carefully on crooked cobblestones. Walkers can even climb down to the coast. Small bars and cafés supply drinks and snacks. When you look closely at the sheer rock walls, it is difficult to imagine just how people can survive here. In fact until well into the last century many villagers emigrated to Latin America to escape the grinding poverty. Fortunately, those days are over. Tourism now provides a good living. But what is a surprise is to see so many orange and lemon trees thriving on the meticulously landscaped terraces. For a good part of the way, a narrow ribbon of asphalt winds its way through the mountains. Occasionally, you will catch sight of the sea down below.

When you've crossed a pass, strong winds will herald the proximity of the north coast, and before long the village of **Buenavista del Norte** → p. 36 will appear in front of you. The lonely TF-445 now runs from there below cliffs to the far northwest corner of Tenerife. Take care when the weather is bad. Rockfalls are not uncommon after heavy rain. Often the road is officially closed. If you wish to continue, you do so at your own risk. As you drive along this road, it's easy to see that the region around Buena Vista, and the **Punta de Teno** → p. 36,

Masca – a beautiful little village in a remarkable mountain setting

the destination of this detour, originated from massive lava flows that rolled down from the interior of the island and created new land. The journey comes to an end just below the two lighthouses – the old one is only visible from the small stony beach on the right-hand side of the road. The wind constantly blows here. In the sheltered bay on the left below you, however, it etches bizarre figures on the almost totally smooth surface of the water. When the weather is clear, the neighbouring island of La Palma is visible to the northwest.

After so much untrammeled nature, you will soon find yourself in a friendlier place. After a twenty-minute journey, you will see Garachico → p. 33 ahead of you. When, in 1706, the Montaña Negra in the Teide region erupted, large parts of this major commercial port were swept away. As if by a miracle, only the tiny fort and some fine colonial homes were spared. These relics still form the Old Town, a splendid example of Tenerife's traditional architecture. From the several restaurants in the town, choose one which serves proper Canarian-style fare. Fresh fish and seafood are served every day.

So now, suitably revived, continue on the TF-42 to Icod de los Vinos → p. 38, where you will find the Drago Milenario, one of Tenerife's most recognised symbols. Leave your car in the large, signposted car-park and walk the last few metres on foot. Just after El Tanque → p. 38 on your way back to Puerto de Santiago on the TF-82, you will find a 'camel centre'. In fact the animals are dromedaries, but that does not detract from the fun of riding on the back of one of these single-humped beasts of burden. From there it's a straightforward run back to your starting point. As the sun sets, a gleaming Mount Teide remains a constant companion to your left.

3 FROM THE SOUTH UP TO THE NATIONAL PARK

Just a few kilometres beyond the main holiday resorts in the south are some magnificent mountainous landscapes. First of all you pass sweet-scented pine forests with views out to sea and to neighbouring islands, then the striking volcanic cones on the huge of Las Cañadas escarpment come into view. You will eventually arrive at the bizarre stony wasteland of Teide National Park, where you can join the 'Perfect Route'. After that, it's back across fields of more recent volcanic clinker.

From Los Cristianos/Playa de las Américas → p. 85 follow the TF-51 towards Arona. Before you reach the little town, which is also the administrative centre for the holiday region, it is worth making a stop at the Finca del Arte in Chayofa (signposted), where contemporary art is exhibited in what used to be a tomato warehouse. If you're travelling with children, then you might like to pay a visit to the jungle zoo, the Parque de Águilas→ p. 109. Shortly after you will arrive in Arona → p. 91, which boasts an attractive historic core , dominated by the table-top Roque del Conde.

The road then winds up through cultivated terraces. Passing fruit orchards, vineyards and potato fields, you will finally reach Vilaflor → p. 77, Spain's highest mountain village. All the main places of interest are around the main square: shops selling the local lace, restaurants serving traditional food; there is also an interesting parish church honouring San Pedro, a native of Vilaflor, and Tenerife's one and only saint.

A few kilometres higher up, gnarled, centuries-old giant pines mark the start of a large *pinar* – the name for the Canarian forests, where this indigenous variety (Pinus canariensis) grows. ⅍ On a clear day you can often catch, between the branches of the trees, a glimpse of the neighbouring islands of La Gomera and El Hierro. At the km 65 marker, a rutted track leads off to the Paisaje Lunar → p. 77, bizarre cones and towers formed out of the tufa rock over thousands of years. A little higher up is the popular INSIDER TIP Las Lajas picnic site. Not only is it a haunt of birders, there is also a snack bar here, but opening times are rather irregular. After a few more kilometres, you will pass the Boca de Tauce, the

Paisaje Lunar – perhaps a little too green for a lunar landscape, but even so ...

name for this breach in the caldera rim. It also forms a natural gateway to the Las Cañadas arena.

At this point you can link up with the 'Perfect Route' → p. 30. The tour described here, however, takes you to the left on the TF 38, passing the ☀ Mirador Chío, from which you can survey the fields of black cinders left behind after the 1799 eruption of the Pico Viejo. On the right, next to the 'Old Peak', you will see the only slightly higher Mount Teide → p. 70. As you continue, you will drive past open expanses of black, solidified lava, before the road starts to wind its way down over the foothills of Las Cañadas. Initially you will see small, rather delicate pine trees clinging on to the inhospitable lava soil, but before much older stands of pine forest take

over. Rays of sunshine pierce through the long needles. When the weather is bad and veils of cloud get trapped in the branches of the trees, the landscape can take on a ghostly, mysterious air. The first village you reach after so much exposure to the natural world is Chío. Don't expect to find anything exciting here, but it may be worthwhile taking a brief stop to peep inside the ☺ Delicias del Sol, a shop, where you can buy delicious marmalades, chutneys, cakes, biscuits, wine and liqueurs. Almost everything is home-made from organic ingredients. From Chío you descend to the coast and Puerto de Santiago → p. 93; alternatively, you can follow the TF-82 at a mid-altitude to Adeje → p. 90, finishing off the tour with a short excursion up the Barranco del Infierno → p. 90

SPORTS & ACTIVITIES

As the northeast trade winds sweep reliably along Tenerife's coasts, wind-surfing has become the most popular of the many different water sports. Bodysurfing off Playa de las Américas has become very popular too.

There are tennis and squash courts in all the holiday resorts. Sports equipment is available for hire on-site. But there are other activities, such as deep-sea fishing and go-karting. Major sporting events staged annually include the two sailing regattas, Copa del Cabildo in March and the Trofeo Infanta SAR Cristina in November, and also the Vuelta Ciclista Isla de Tenerife round-the-island cycle race in September.

CYCLING

Among elite professional road racers, Tenerife has become very popular because of the steep hill climbs and the mild winter climate. Leisure cyclists, who are likely to be deterred by the gradients, will find flat roads by the coast, particularly in the south, but they will have to share the highways with a lot of traffic. However, Spanish motorists are traditionally respectful of cyclists. Please note: a helmet is compulsory for cyclists in Spain. Mountain-bikers are allowed to go off-road.

If you are in one of the holiday resorts, to hire a cycle for a day will cost from 14 euros, for a week from 71 euros, e.g. from *Diga Sports | Playa de las Americas*

Photo: Windsurfers off El Médano

Hang-gliding, windsurfing, walking – if you love the outdoor life, there's sure to be something here for you

Avenida Rafael Puig 23 | tel. 9 22 79 30 09 | www.digasports.co.uk. Guided tours start at 46 euros.

Even away from the main holiday towns, cycle enthusiasts will usually find the facilities they need.

DIVING

Diving schools offer courses and also trips to some truly amazing underwater sites – not too far from the coast. Snorkelers exploring the inshore waters will

catch a glimpse of a few small fish, but accompanied scuba divers will be able to see barracudas, parrot fish, mantas, tuna and, if they're lucky, even whales and dolphins. There is such an abundance of fish in the waters around Tenerife, and that includes not just Atlantic, but also sub-tropical species. Off *Los Cristianos*, for example, you can see coral reefs, observe skate near *Las Galletas* and on the seabed near *Puerto de la Cruz* dive into volcanic caves. Night-time and cave diving is possible; one unusual, underwater sight nearby is **INSIDER TIP** the wreckage of an airplane. All diving schools offer PADI certification.

The *Centro de Buceo Atlantik* in *Puerto de la Cruz*, (tel. *9 22 36 28 01*) and *Playa de las Américas (tel. 9 22 71 79 11 | www. scubacanarias.com)* runs courses from 240 euros, courses for beginners 75 euros. The *Barakuda Club Tenerife* in *Playa Paraíso* organises a wide range of diving

Downhill can be harder than uphill – walking in Teide National Park

tours *(tel. 9 22 74 18 81 | www.teneriffa-tauchen.de)*. The same applies to the *Aqua-Marina Dive Centre* in *Playa de las Américas* near the Playa de las Vistas *(Local 396A | C.C. Compostela Beach | tel. 9 22 79 79 44 | www.aquamarinadiving tenerife.com)*.

GOLF

Golfers can putt and tee off from three 27-hole, four 18-hole and two 9-hole golf courses throughout the year. Anyone can use them upon payment of the green fee (details can be found under Sport & Leisure in the various regional chapters).

HANG-GLIDING

Hang-gliding and paragliding are both very popular. There are no fewer than 40 different take-off points on the island. The best one, *Izaña,* lies on the *Cumbre Dorsal* at a height of 2,350m (7,710ft) behind the observatory. But training and equipment are only available at Spanish-speaking clubs. *www.clubparapenteizana.com*

RIDING

There are several riding stables in the south of Tenerife. The *Amarilla Golf & Country Club* near *Los Abrigos* has its own stables. Several fincas specialise in riding holidays. The *Finca Estrella* near Icod de los Vinos *(Fuente de Vega 24 | tel. 9 22 81 43 82 | www.teneriffa-reiten. com)* offers riding lessons and all-in holiday packages with accommodation. The *Centro Hípico los Brezos (tel. 9 22 56 72 22 | info@hipicalosbrezos.net)* near *Tacoronte* offers hacks in the still unspoilt woodland nearby. At the *Centro Hípico Alcalá* in the southwest of the island, you can learn and/or practise classic and Western riding, including dressage and showjumping; riding shows including dancing horses in the evening *(about 500m beyond the edge of Alcalá to the south | www.centrohipicodealcala.com)*.

SURFING

Surfers will find excellent opportunities on the north coast, however, the best place on the island is *Playa de Benijo* behind the Anaga Mountains, but the journey there can take a long time. A good spot for beginners is the *Playa de Martiánez* in Puerto de la Cruz, but surfers wanting more challenging waves are likely to make for the *Playa del Socorro* or the *Playa Punta Brava* west of Puerto de la Cruz. The conditions are often ideal off *El Médano* in the south.

WALKING

Tenerife is a paradise for walkers. There are well over twenty regions on the island where walkers will find trails of all lengths and levels of difficulty. But always popular are the *Barranco del Infierno*, the *Valle de la Orotava*, the *Anaga Mountains* and the *Parque Nacional del Teide.* Walking independently can pose problems, because the island maps are not sufficiently detailed. Furthermore, many of the trails are poorly signposted or even dangerous, especially if the weather turns or it suddenly gets dark. An up-to-date walking guide is advisable, but a rucksack with water and emergency rations is essential. Inexperienced walkers may wish to join a walk led by an experienced guide.

Tenerife Hiking is one company that offers guided walks. Walks can be tailored to level of fitness or to meet particular requests. Guides are fluent in English and Spanish. Food and water are supplied or, if requested, a meal in a typical Canarian restaurant can be arranged. *(Tenerife Outdoors | Calle Vistabella, Acojeja, Guía de Isora, Santa Cruz de Tenerife | tel. 922 85 24 96 | www.tenerifeoutdoors.com).* Diga Sports is another company with plenty of experience in organising walking and adventure activities – there's something for all levels of fitness *(Playa de las Americas | Avenida Rafael Puig 23 | tel. 9 22 79 30 09 | www.digasports. co.uk).* For more information about the companies that organise walking tours, ask in one of the tourist offices.

WINDSURFING

The hot spots are mainly along the southeast coast – with wind strengths in winter usually around 5, in summer as high as 8, experienced windsurfers love it here. *El Cabezo* and La Jaquita (wind strengths 4–8) are recommended only for experts; every year world championship events are staged in the inshore waters near *El Médano* (wind strengths 3–5). If you feel like giving windsurfing a try, the more sheltered conditions off *Playa de las Americas* and along the west coast are much more favourable for novices.

Surfing the Atlantic waves is never easy

TRAVEL WITH KIDS

Younger guests are important guests. The main resort hotels have their own pools, play areas, sometimes supervised, sometimes with entertainers (check when booking). Los Cristianos and Los Gigantes both boast beaches that are perfect for children.

In many places, on 5 January, the day before Epiphany – *Los Reyes Magos* – there are INSIDER TIP children's parades, likewise during Carnaval (ask at the tourist office for information).

THE NORTHWEST

LAGO DE MARTIÁNEZ ●
(128 C1) (*ØØ H4*)

Puerto de la Cruz is by far the most popular resort on Tenerife's north coast,

but it doesn't have many good beaches. Also, as the Atlantic Ocean can unleash some powerful forces against the playas, children cannot swim safely here. César Manrique, the brilliant architect and landscape architect from Lanzarote, came up with a solution. In 1977 he designed this complex, which is known variously as Lido San Telmo, Lago de Martiánez or Costa Martiánez. It consists of four saltwater pools and a large central 'lake' at different levels, but there are also waterfalls, fountains, cafeterias and a restaurant. Islands of lava rock and lush greenery create an aquatic park like no other. For children there are climbing frames, a bright red, walk-in grotto area and they just love the warm Jacuzzi pool. Suitable for children from eight years of

Parrots in the park, an aqua paradise and hands-on science – it doesn't always have to be sandcastles on the beach

age. Daily 10am–5pm | Admission adults 3.50 euros, children 1.10 euros | Costa Martiánez

LORO PARQUE ★
(128 B1) (*G–H4*)

This vast zoo is one of Tenerife's main tourist attractions. It is situated at the end of the Playa Jardín and consists of parks, tropical gardens, animal enclosures, aquariums and arenas for shows and special events. It is said that the park keeps the world's largest collection of parrots in one place; among the approx. 350 species and 4,000 animals are some very rare specimens bred by the keepers at the Loro Parque.

For many years the park has kept other animals – from bats to tigers and from crocodiles to gorillas. A panoramic cinema shows how a bird views the world. But even better is the ‚Katandra': a huge outdoor aviary, where visitors can climb up ladders and suspension bridges to the tree-tops to see a wide range of exotic feathered friends at close quarters.

Some 200 creatures, notably king and rockhopper penguins, live in the world's largest penguinarium at temperatures around freezing point. It's all beneath a huge dome, from which a constant shower of man-made snow descends.

For another close-up of the animal kingdom, explore the huge perspex cylinder, home to around 20,000 fish. Dolphin and sea lion shows are staged to entertain the visitors and in an underwater tunnel fierce sharks and manta rays can be observed in a near-natural habitat. The orcas are another major attraction. Killer whales, all of which were born in captivity, have their own show.

The enclosures are of exemplary quality. If all of the above is not enough, there is an African market, a Thai village, an orchid house, plus restaurants and cafeterias and lots more. Suitable for children over four years of age.

Daily 8.30am–4pm (last entry) | Admission 32 euros, children (4–11) 21 euros, discount on second visit; combined ticket with Siam Park 52 and 35 euros respectively | Playa Punta Brava (free mini-train every 20 mins from Playa de Martiánez) | www.loroparque.com

THE NORTHEAST

MUSEO DE LA CIENCIA Y EL COSMOS
(130 B3) (*M3*)

Interactive displays and easy-to-understand examples in this Science Museum in La Laguna help children from about eight years of age to learn through play about the universe, the earth and man. Most exhibits with explanations in Eng-

Making contact in the Loro Parque – 'Give us a kiss', says the dolphin to young Miguel

lish. *Tue–Sun 9am–7pm | Admission 3 euros, Sun free | Avenida de los Menceyes 70 | www.museosdetenerife.org*

PARQUE MARÍTIMO CÉSAR-MANRIQUE (130 C4) (*ID N3*)

The open-air water park in the capital was built to a design by architect César Manrique – with several swimming pools, a large children's pool, islands of volcanic rock and large open areas for sunbathing. Small cafeterias serve drinks and snacks. *Daily 10am–5pm | Admission 3 euros, children 1.50 euros | Avenida de la Constitución 5*

THE SOUTHWEST

AQUALAND (136 C4) (*ID E4*)

A saltwater theme park with pools, water slides and flumes, waterfalls and the slow-flowing Congo River, so you can drift gently through the whole complex. Dolphinarium with daily shows, play areas. Plus snack bars and shops. You will have to pay extra for loungers, etc. and shows. Recommended for families with children over three years of age. *Daily 10am–5pm | Admission 19.50 euros, children (3–12 years) 13 euros | San Eugenio Alto, Autopista del Sur, exit 29 | www.aqualand.es/tenerife*

EL LAGUILLO (132 B5) (*ID C8*)

This small, open-air pool with a café makes a good alternative to the beach in *Los Gigantes*. *Daily 9.30am–5.30pm | Admission 4.50 euros, children under 8 years of age 2.75 euros | Ticket for a week 20 and 11 euros respectively, lounger included*

PARQUE LAS ÁGUILAS (137 D4) (*ID E11*)

This vast jungle park spread over 7 hectares (17 acres) of lush vegetation, lakes and waterfalls, plus many different birds

of prey. Watch eagles, vultures, falcons, owls and other raptors at feeding time and also on the hunt for prey. But it's not just an aviary. The park has an amazing collection of white tigers, lions, leopards, penguins, pelicans, marabou storks, hippos, crocodiles and orangutans. And then there is a cactus garden, climbing equipment and pedalos on a mini-lake, plus a snack-bar and pizzeria. *Daily 10am–4.30pm | Admission 24 euros, 16.50 euros | Directions: Carretera Los Cristianos–Arona, km 4 marker | Free buses from the town | www.aguilas junglepark.com*

SIAM PARK ★ (136 C5) (*ID E11*)

The newest attraction in the south is a themed aquapark, the theme being old Thailand. Extending over an area of 14 hectares (34 acres), you can view temples, encounter giant dragons and shop in a market on stilts, then there are all the water park thrills, which includes eight waterslides, one of which, the Tower of Power, is only for the very brave. There's an almost vertical drop before you whoosh through a clear plastic tube in a shark tank. Surging waves three metres high from the Wave Palace eventually reach a man made bay with a white sandy beach. Younger children will love the 'Lost City', an adventure playground in water. Towers are linked by bridges and nets, waterfalls, fountains and gentle slides. But the highlight is a hollow giant's head that fills with water. Once it has filled up, it tilts over, its contents plummeting in a powerful waterfall – much to the delight of the children. Suitable for children from three years of age. *Daily 10am–5pm | Admission 30 euros , children 19.50 euros, combined ticket with Loro Parque 49 and 33 euros respectively | Autopista del Sur, exit 28 | www.siampark.net*

FESTIVALS & EVENTS

Practically every day of the year some-where on Tenerife, there will be a parade, a pilgrimage or some other religious festival. But there is good reason for this, as the island has always been pitilessly exposed to the forces of nature, whether sea or volcano. Each village has its own patron saint. The Catholic celebrations of Easter and Corpus Christi take the form of pilgrimages. At farmers' festivals and other traditional events a parade of beautifully decorated ox carts usually get things off to a colourful start. Then the partying gets going with dancing and feasting. But it's not all about the past – music and ballet evenings in Santa Cruz or rock and folk festivals in La Laguna demonstrate that the island is still very much part of mainstream European culture. But the annual Carnaval has to be the wildest north of Rio.

PUBLIC HOLIDAYS

1 Jan: New Year's Day *(Año Nuevo)*; **6 Jan:** Epiphany *(Los Reyes)*; **19 March:** St Joseph's Day *(San José)*; **March/April:** Good Friday *(Viernes Santo)*; **1 May:** May Day (Día del Trabajo); **30 May:** Canary Islands Day *(Día de las Islas Canarias)*; **May/June:** Corpus Christi; **25 July:** St James' Day *(Santiago Apóstol)*; **15 Aug:** Assumption of the Blessed Virgin *(Asunción)*; **12 Oct:** Columbus Day *(Día de la Hispanidad)*; **1 Nov:** All Saints Day *(Todos los Santos)*; **6 Dec:** Constitution Day *(Día de la Constitución)*; **8 Dec:** Immaculate Conception *(Immaculada Concepción)*; **25 Dec:** Christmas *(Navidad)*

FESTIVALS & EVENTS

JANUARY/FEBRUARY

For a whole month, Santa Cruz de Tenerife hosts the ▶ *Festival de Música de Canarias*, where music from all over the world, and that's everything from chamber music to philharmonic concerts, is performed in the Teatro Guimerá or in the Auditorio. *www.festivaldecanarias.com*

FEBRUARY/MARCH

Wild celebrations in the weeks before Lent – the whole island, but in particular Santa Cruz and Puerto de la Cruz, go overboard for the ▶ ★ *Carnaval*. It culminates in processions and dance festivals in Santa Cruz de Tenerife.

MARCH/APRIL

Magnificent ▶ *processions* take place during the whole of Easter week, but with all eyes on La Laguna. The climax is a series of doleful processions on Good Friday.

The climax is the Carnaval extravaganza – but solemn religious festivals also feature in Tenerife's events calendar

MAY

▶ *Fiesta de San Isidro:* Celebrations take place around the 15 May in honour of the patron saint of farmers: in Araya, Granadilla, Los Realejos and La Orotava. The locals dress up in traditional costume and dance to music played on Canarian instruments.

MAY/JUNE

More processions to mark ▶ ⭐ *Corpus Christi* – the best ones are in La Laguna and La Orotava. Magnificent flower carpets and coloured volcanic sand are laid out on the streets and squares.

JULY

On the second Sunday in June the ▶ *Fiesta y Romería del San Benito Abad* is celebrated with a pilgrimage and grand fair to honour the patron saint of La Laguna. 25 July is ▶ *St James' Day (Santiago Apóstol)* and another occasion for a party. ▶ *Nuestra Señora del Carmen,* the patron saint of fishermen, is remembered on 16 July with processions of boats in Santa Cruz de Tenerife and Puerto de la Cruz.

AUGUST

▶ INSIDER TIP The Romería de la Virgen *de Candelaria* is an important day on the island. On 15 August tens of thousands of pilgrims make their way to Candelaria to pay homage to the island's patron saint. On the next day the people of Garachico let their hair down for the ▶ *Romería de San Roque*, a classic farmer's festival with lively processions. Also in the outlying communities.

SEPTEMBER

As part of the ▶ *Fiestas del Cristo* the best folk music bands in the Canaries gather in La Laguna for the two-day ▶ INSIDER TIP *Festival Sabandeño*, an event very popular with young people.

NOVEMBER

Every two years *(next date: 2013)* the island stages ▶ *Festival Foto-Noviembre*, a forum for internationally-renowned photographers to display their work. The main centres are Santa Cruz and La Laguna *(www.fotonoviembre.com)*.

LINKS, BLOGS, APPS & MORE

LINKS

▶ www.todotenerife.es The official information site with an excellent translation into English. Published by the Tenerife Island Council, it aims to offer 'a cultural, social, historical and organisational overview of the island'

▶ www.tenerife-information-centre.com Pages and pages of useful information written by a long-term resident in an easy-to-read style. Regularly updated

▶ www.iter.es The 🕙 Instituto Tecnológico y de Energias Renovables (ITER) explains in English how the island is addressing green issues, e.g. solar panels, wind farms, bioclomatic housing

▶ www.tenerifeweather.info Is the sun going to keep shining?

▶ There are countless websites for English-speaking visitors. Here are just a few: www.islandconnections.eu, www.tenerife-uncovered.com, www.tenerifeguide.com, www.spain-tenerife.com, www.insighttenerife.com

▶ www.panoramio.com A photo-sharing website linked to Google maps. Enter the place you want to visit in the search box and then take a peep at other people's holiday snaps

BLOGS & FORUMS

▶ www.tenerifeforum.org Probably the liveliest online site for the island. There's a forum, blog and news page. Click on Today's Posts for a taster.

▶ www.expat-blog.com/en/destination/europe/spain/tenerife There is a large contingent of expatriate Brits on Tenerife. Pictures, classified ads and a very lively forum. If you need specific information, then best to ask someone who lives there. Also helpful if planning to relocate

▶ www.tenerife-information-centre.com (see above) also a has some interesting blogs

Regardless of whether you are still preparing your trip or already in Tenerife: these addresses will provide you with more information, videos and networks to make your holiday even more enjoyable

VIDEOS, RADIO & PODCASTS

► www.elviajero.elpais.com/videos/canarias Search the website for Spain's biggest-circulation daily newspaper and you will find a variety of videos on the island's most interesting features, e.g. Puerto de la Cruz (in Spanish)

► www.airammusical.com Watch a trailer for the Flamenco musical at the Pirámide de *Arona*

► Oasis Radio – Podcasts available (100.8–101 FM); Power FM – Audio on demand (91.1–91.9 FM); or Coast FM (89.2 FM). Or listen live from anywhere in the world online

► www.notesinspanish.com Download Spanish lessons to your mp3

APPS

► Download the app TenerifeWebcam to your Android smartphone and see your holiday destination live

► Star Walk Point your iPhone at the sky above Tenerife. Sensors work out your viewing direction and identify the stars above. Star Chart does the same on Android phones

► Suntimer This app helps you to calculate the time that you can lie in the sun without harm

► The Kite and Windsurfing Navigator Up-to-date forecasts and wind alerts for water sports enthusiasts

► NearestWiki GPS identifies where you are and then sends you Wikipedia pages with all the background information on your current location

NETWORKS

► www.gonomad.com The travellers' bible. Globetrotters supply information on subjects such as Women's Travel, Unique Lodgings or Unusual Tours

► www.turismodecanarias.com Another website with masses of information about the Canary Islands. Best feature is Zone 2.0. The Video section is devoted to YouTube clips, Social Networks has links to gay groups, and there are more blogs

TRAVEL TIPS

ARRIVAL

✈ Cheap flights are available from the UK and Ireland with Ryanair, easyJet and Thomas Cook (UK flight time from approx. 4 hours). Flights with no hotel booking cost between 300 and 500 euros. Scheduled flights are much more expensive and nearly always involve a stopover. There are no direct flights from the USA. There are two airports: the southern airport, Reina Sofía, which is served by most international airlines, is a 20-minute drive from Playa de las Américas and Los Cristianos and about 1 hour from Puerto de la Cruz. Scheduled buses run from Playa de las Américas (nos. 111, 340, 343; 2.50 euros), Santa Cruz de Tenerife (no. 11; 7 euros) and Puerto de la Cruz (no. 340; 11 euros). Taxis to Los Cristianos/Playa de las Américas cost 20–30 euros, to Puerto de Santiago approx. 45 euros and to Puerto de la Cruz 90–120 euros. All scheduled flights and many low-cost airlines land at Tenerife Norte airport near La Laguna. For flight information call *9 22 63 59 99*. Inter-Canary Island flights depart from here and also from *Reina Sofía (Information tel. 9 22 75 90 00)*.

🚢 Once a week at 5pm a car ferry operated by Compañía Trasmediterránea-Acciona leaves from the southern Spanish port of Cádiz. The crossing to Santa Cruz de Tenerife takes 31 hours (return trip also once a week). A fare for a single journey starts from 269 euros per person (in a 4-bed cabin). A car costs 255 euros. Tickets can be booked through travel agencies.

BUSES & TRAM

Buses on Tenerife are called guaguas (pronounced uahuah). Santa Cruz's central bus station, *Estación de Guaguas*, is on Avenida 3 de Mayo 47. Green TITSA buses run from here to almost every town on Tenerife. Nos. 103 and 110 are express buses. You can buy a *Bono-Bus* ticket at bus stations in Santa Cruz and other holiday resorts for 12–30 euros. This gives holders a 25 percent reduction on all fares. *Information is available in Spanish and English on 9 22 53 13 00 Mon–Fri 7am–9pm* and also on the internet at *www.titsa.com*.
Since 2007 a tram service *(tranvía)* has been in operation between Santa Cruz and La Laguna. It only costs 2.45 euros for a journey of 12km (8 miles) from the tram stop near Santa Cruz's Plaza de España to the university town *(www.tranviatenerife.com)*.

CAMPING

Wild camping is not allowed on Tenerife. But there are four campsites:

RESPONSIBLE TRAVEL

It doesn't take a lot to be environmentally friendly whilst travelling. Don't just think about your carbon footprint whilst flying to and from your holiday destination but also about how you can protect nature and culture abroad. As a tourist it is especially important to respect nature, look out for local products, cycle instead of driving, save water and much more. If you would like to find out more about eco-tourism please visit: *www.ecotourism.org*

Camping-Caravaning Nauta (Cañada Blanca | Ctra 6225, km 1.5 | Las Galletas, Arona | tel. 9 22 78 51 18); Camping El Castillo de Himeche S. L. (Guía de Isora | tel. 6 86 25 89 54); Camping Playa de la Arena (Tacoronte | tel. 6 69 81 15 35); Camping Montaña Roja (El Médano | TF-643 km 3 | tel. 9 22 17 99 03 | www.tenerifecampingplaya.com).

Free use of the public campsites in the mountains, some of which are in very attractive spots in the mountains (with or without sanitary facilities) is allowed with the prior permission of the *Oficina de Medio Ambiente* in *La Laguna (Calle Las Macetas Pabellón Santiago Martín | tel. 9 22 23 91 99).* If you have a caravan, it is permitted to spend at least one night on public car-parks or on the street, in remote spots longer.

CAR HIRE

Car rental companies run offices in the airports, in all the holiday resorts and also in many hotels. The hire charges for a small car could well be less than 20 euros per day (including taxes and fully comprehensive insurance). *Cicar* is a reliable local company, which has bureaux in all airports, ports and holiday resorts. The cars are well maintained, but in the event of a breakdown roadside assistance arrives promptly *(tel. 9 28 82 29 00 | www.cicar.com).*

As a general rule remember that the rental car must have a high-visibility vest on board. All-terrain vehicles, trikes and motorcycles, which you can also rent everywhere, are considerably more expensive.

CLIMATE & WHEN TO GO

Tenerife's mild climate means only small fluctuations in temperature. In the arid south, even in winter, temperatures hardly ever fall below 18 °C and only rarely rise above 24 °C. In summer, however, the temperature can stay at 30 °C and above for weeks. Even at moderate altitudes weak air currents can give rise to an oppressive heat. The temperatures in the northeast are often significantly lower than in the south. At over 500m above sea level at night and in winter it can be quite cold. So remember to pack not just a hat and a sweater, but also a cagoule. As water temperatures in Tenerife are always in the 18 ° to 24 °C range, it's fine to swim in the sea any day of the year. The best time to visit the island is from November to March.

BUDGETING

Taxis	from 0.50 £ / 0.80 $ per kilometre / basic pick-up charge 2.00 euros
Coffee	from 0.80 £ / 1.30 $ for a cup of coffee
Souvenir	1.25 £ / 2 $ for one strelitzia plant
Wine	from 1.25 £ / 2 $ for a glass (0.2l)
Petrol	just over 0.80 £ / 1.30 $ for 1 l of unleaded
Tapa	from 2 £ / 3.30 $ for a small snack

CONSULATES & EMBASSIES

UK CONSULATE
Mon–Fri 8.30am–1.30pm | Plaza Weyler, 8, 1° | 38003 Santa Cruz de Tenerife | tel. 9 02 10 93 56| email Tenerife.Consulate@ fco.gov.uk

US CONSULATE
Edificio ARCA | C/ Los Martínez Escobar, 3, Oficina 7 | 35007 Las Palmas | tel. 928 27 12 59

CUSTOMS

Although Spain is in the EU, there are restrictions when returning to the UK and the USA from the Canary Islands for anyone over 17 years of age. Maximum amounts are 200 cigarettes or 50 cigars or 250 grams of tobacco, 1 litre of spirits, 2 litres of wine, 50 g of perfume, 250 cl of Eau de Cologne.

DRIVING

The roads on Tenerife are good and safe. Maximum speed: in urban areas 50 km/h (30 mph), on country roads 90 km/h (56 mph) and on motorways 120 km/h (75 mph). A driver with a blood alcohol level of 0.5 grams per litre (or, a blood alcohol level of 0.15 grams per litre in the case of a driver who has had a licence for two years or less) can expect harsh penalties and a driving ban. Drivers must also keep a high-visibility jacket in the car.
Parking is not allowed where there are red and yellow markings by the kerb; a parking fee is payable where there are blue lines.

EMERGENCY CALLS

There is one number for all emergencies: *112*.

HEALTH

The greatest risk for tourists is high exposure to the sun (even in winter). So sunburnt skin, particularly at the start of the holiday, is a frequent, but avoidable occurrence. A sunscreen with high sun protection factor (from 15) should there-

SPA HOTELS

Tenerife has been a favoured destination for those in need of rest and convalescence since the end of the 19th century. The island has built up a fine reputation in that field, but now that kind of establishment has been rebranded. They now call themselves spa hotels and offer a wide range of services including complementary medicine, Far Eastern therapies, pamper weeks and beauty treatments. Standing out from the crowd in Puerto de la Cruz are the *Oriental Spa Garden* in the *Hotel Botánico (www.hotelbotanico. com)* and the smaller spa in the *Bahía Príncipe San Felipe (www.bahia-principe. com). The Océano (www.oceano-tenerife. com)* in Punta del Hidalgo describes itself as a vitality hotel and medical spa and offers a wide variety of treatments.

To the south in Playa de las Américas is the classic spa hotel, the *Mare Nostrum Spa (www.marenostrumspa.es)*. Nearby is the only spa independent of a hotel, the *Aqua Club Termal (www.aquaclubtermal.com)* – highly recommended. The *Thai Zen SPAce* in the *Hotel El Mirador* by the Bahía del Duque *(www.elmirador-granhotel.com)* offers 'care for the body and soul' and the spa in the Sheraton La Caleta (www.sheraton lacaleta.com) has a range of exclusive spa packages. If you want a sumptuous pamper package in an elegant setting, then maybe the *Abama Hotel* is for you – fine views over the lush golf-course and tall palms, plus lots of timber features *(www.abama hotelresort.com)*. All spas and their facilities are open to non-residents.

fore be applied every day. Some form of head wear is also important.

DOCTORS & HOSPITALS

If you have a European Health Insurance Card (EHIC), you will be treated free of charge by doctors, outpatient clinics and hospitals, which are part of the Spanish Seguridad Social system. Otherwise, you should request a detailed invoice *(factura)*, so that you can claim a refund from your holiday insurance company.

Santa Cruz de Tenerife: *Hospital Nuestra Señora de la Candelaria | 24-hour service | Carretera Rosario 145 | Tel. 60 9 22 20 00 Hospiten Rambla | La Rambla 115 | tel. 22 29 16 00 9 | www.hospiten.es*

Playa de las Américas/Los Cristianos: *Salus Medical Centre | 24-hour service | Playa de las Américas | Avenida República Panamá 3 | tel. 9 22 79 12 53 Hospiten Sur, 24-hour service and hotel visits | Calle Siete Islas 8 | tel. 9 22 75 00 22 | www.hospiten.es*

Puerto de la Cruz: *Salus Medical Centre | 24-hour service | Calle Valois 43 | tel.9. 22 37 32 02*

Puerto de Santiago/Los Gigantes: *Salus Medical Centre | 24-hour Service | Avenida Maritima 43 | tel. 9 22 86 04 32*

PHARMACIES

Pharmacies *(farmacias)* are recognisable by the green Maltese cross (Mon–Fri 9am–1pm and 4pm–7pm, Sat 9am–1pm). The sign Farmacia de Guardia will give the address of the nearest duty pharmacy.

INFORMATION BEFORE YOU GO

SPANISH NATIONAL TOURISM OFFICES
Tourist information is available from the Spanish tourism offices and also at *www. spain.info*
- *6th Floor 64 North Row | London W1K 7DE | info.londres@tourspain.es*
– *1395 Brickell Avenue, Suite 1130 | Miami, FL 33131 | oetmiami@tourspain.es*
– *845 North Michigan Av, Suite 915-E | Chicago, IL 60611 | chicago@tourspain.es*
– *8383 Wilshire Blvd., Suite 956 | Beverly Hills, CA 90211 | losangeles@tourspain.es*
– *60 East 42nd Street, Suite 5300 (53rd Floor) | New York, NY 10165-0039 | nuevayork@tourspain.es*

INFORMATION ON TENERIFE

REINA SOFÍA AIRPORT
Arrivals hall; Mon–Fri 9am–9pm | Sat 9am–5pm | tel. 9 22 39 20 37

INTERNET & WLAN

Now hotels in all categories offer a WLAN service. However, these are often not included in the room charge and so must be paid for sometimes at expensive rates (e.g. 10 mins for 1 euro). If you don't have your laptop with you, you may be able to make use of the hotel's internet computer, but again a charge may be payable. A slightly cheaper alternative is an internet café. There will usually be one in the shopping centres in larger resorts. *Salones recreativos, i.e. amusement arcades*, often have a few computer terminals.

NATURIST BEACHES

Naturism is normally only permissible on a few beaches, for example, west of the Montaña Roja near El Médano, on the Playa de Montaña Amarilla (Costa del Silencio) or on the Playa de las Gaviotas near Playa de las Teresitas.

PHONE & MOBILE PHONE

You can phone home with coins or phone cards *(teletarjeta)*, available from post offices and newspaper kiosks. The phone box will be marked *internacional*. A 3-minute call to the UK costs about 2 euros, between 10pm and 8am about 60 cents. It is also cheaper at the weekend (Sat from about 2pm). In many holiday resorts, there are call shops known as *locutorios*, where you pay when the call is over. To call the UK, dial 0044, the USA 001, then the area code but without 0, followed by the subscriber's number. If you wish to phone Tenerife from abroad, the code is 0034, then dial the subscriber's number. When 'roaming' with a mobile phone, choose the cheapest network. If you purchase a prepaid card in the host country, then you will not pay for incoming calls.

On Tenerife you can buy prepaid cards, for providers such as Orange, Movistar and Vodafone, in many places, e.g. tobacconists, newsagents, kiosks, supermarkets and service stations. Don't forget to switch off your mailbox before you leave home – it can prove costly, if you leave it on.

POST

To send a letter or a postcard to other EU countries will cost 0.60 euros. Ideally, packages with valuable contents should be shipped as registered mail *(certificado)*. Stamps may be purchased at the post office *(correos)*. On most of the island post offices are open Mon–Fri 8.30am–2.30pm,

WEATHER IN TENERIFE

	Jan	Feb	March	April	May	June	July	Aug	Sept	Oct	Nov	Dec
Daytime temperatures in °C/°F												
	21/70	21/70	22/72	23/73	24/75	26/79	28/82	29/84	28/82	26/79	23/73	22/72
Nighttime temperatures in °C/°F												
	14/57	14/57	15/59	16/61	17/63	19/66	21/70	21/70	21/70	19/66	17/63	16/61
Sunshine hours/day												
	5	6	7	8	10	11	11	11	9	7	5	5
Precipitation days/month												
	7	5	3	2	1	0	0	0	1	4	6	7
Water temperature in °C/°F												
	19/66	18/64	18/64	18/64	19/66	20/68	21/70	22/72	23/73	23/73	21/70	20/68

but in Santa Cruz de Tenerife and Puerto de la Cruz they stay open until 8.30pm and are also open on Saturday morning.

PRICES

The price you will have to pay for services (e.g. car repairs) is likely to be slightly higher than in the UK or in the US. Food, much of which has to be imported, is invariably dearer than on the European mainland.

RURAL TOURISM

If you go on holiday to Tenerife, you don't have to stay in a hotel or villa complex. There are a number of agencies on the island, which rent out accommodation in the country. There must be more than 50 such places and they range from fincas for 10 persons to a cave. They have usually been fully renovated and are equipped with modern facilities. Prices are generally much lower than a tourist hotel.

The main agency, an organisation supported with EU funds, is *Attur (Asociación Tinerfeña de Turismo Rural)* with over 50 properties *(Mon–Fri 9am–2pm | Santa Cruz de Tenerife | Calle Castillo 41 | tel. 9 22 53 27 33 | www.attur.es).*

SMOKING

In 2011, Spain adopted the strongest anti-smoking laws in the EU. Proprietors risk draconian fines if customers smoke in enclosed public places, i.e. in all restaurants, bars and cafés. Separate smoking rooms are not permissible either. Even smoking outdoors is restricted; for example, smoking a cigarette in close proximity to a children's playground is an offence.

TAXIS

All taxis are licensed and equipped with a taximeter, which must be turned on before each trip. The fare will be based on 60 cents per kilometre plus a basic pick-up charge of at least 2 euros, and then there are surcharges for Sunday and public holidays, at night, journeys to the port and to the airport and also for large items of luggage. If you would like to make an island tour by taxi, make sure you agree the price beforehand.

TIME

Unlike mainland Spain, Tenerife runs on Greenwich Mean Time, so visitors from the UK and Ireland DO NOT need to adjust their watches.

CURRENCY CONVERTER

£	€	€	£
1	1.10	1	0.90
3	3.30	3	2.70
5	5.50	5	4.50
13	14.30	13	11.70
40	44	40	36
75	82.50	75	67.50
120	132	120	108
250	275	250	225
500	550	500	450

$	€	€	$
1	0.70	1	1.40
3	2.10	3	4.20
5	3.50	5	7
13	9.10	13	18.20
40	28	40	56
75	52.50	75	105
120	84	120	168
250	175	250	350
500	350	500	700

For current exchange rates see www.xe.com

USEFUL PHRASES SPANISH

PRONUNCIATION

c	before 'e' and 'i' like 'th' in 'thin'
ch	as in English
g	before 'e' and 'i' like the 'ch' in Scottish 'loch'
gue, gui	like 'get', 'give'
que, qui	the 'u' is not spoken, i.e. 'ke', 'ki'
j	always like the 'ch' in Scottish 'loch'
ll	like 'lli' in 'million'; some speak it like 'y' in 'yet'
ñ	'nj'
z	like 'th' in 'thin'

IN BRIEF

Yes/No/Maybe	sí/no/quizás
Please/Thank you	por favor/gracias
Hello!/Goodbye!/See you	¡Hola!/¡Adiós!/¡Hasta luego!
Good morning!/afternoon!/ evening!/night!	¡Buenos días!/¡Buenos días!/¡Buenas tardes!/¡Buenas noches!
Excuse me, please!	¡Perdona!/¡Perdone!
May I ...?/Pardon?	¿Puedo ...?/¿Cómo dice?
My name is ...	Me llamo ...
What's your name?	¿Cómo se llama usted?/¿Cómo te llamas?
I'm from ...	Soy de ...
I would like to .../Have you got ...?	Querría .../¿Tiene usted ...?
How much is ...?	¿Cuánto cuesta ...?
I (don't) like that	Esto (no) me gusta.
good/bad/broken/doesn't work	bien/mal/roto/no funciona
too much/much/little/all/nothing	demasiado/mucho/poco/todo/nada
Help!/Attention!/Caution!	¡Socorro!/¡Atención!/¡Cuidado!
ambulance/police/fire brigade	ambulancia/policía/bomberos
May I take a photo here	¿Podría fotografiar aquí?

DATE & TIME

Monday/Tuesday/Wednesday	lunes/martes/miércoles
Thursday/Friday/Saturday	jueves/viernes/sábado
Sunday/working day/holiday	domingo/laborable/festivo
today/tomorrow/yesterday	hoy/mañana/ayer

¿Hablas español?

"Do you speak Spanish?" This guide will help you to say the basic words and phrases in Spanish

hour/minute/second/moment	hora/minuto/segundo/momento
day/night/week/month/year	día/noche/semana/mes/año
now/immediately/before/after	ahora/enseguida/antes/después
What time is it?	¿Qué hora es?
It's three o'clock/It's half past three	Son las tres/Son las tres y media
a quarter to four/a quarter past four	cuatro menos cuarto/ cuatro y cuarto

TRAVEL

open/closed/opening times	abierto/cerrado/horario
entrance / exit	entrada/acceso salida
departure/arrival	salida/llegada
toilets/ladies/gentlemen	aseos/señoras/caballeros
free/occupied	libre/ocupado
(not) drinking water	agua (no) potable
Where is ?/Where are ...?	¿Dónde está ...? /¿Dónde están ...?
left/right	izquierda/derecha
straight ahead/back	recto/atrás
close/far	cerca/lejos
traffic lights/corner/crossing	semáforo/esquina/cruce
bus/tram/U-underground/taxi/cab	autobús/tranvía/metro/taxi
bus stop/cab stand	parada/parada de taxis
parking lot/parking garage	parking/garaje
street map/map	plano de la ciudad/mapa
train station/harbour/airport	estación/puerto/aeropuerto
ferry/quay	transbordador/muelle
schedule/ticket/supplement	horario/billete/suplemento
single/return	sencillo/ida y vuelta
train/track/platform	tren/vía/andén
delay/strike	retraso/huelga
I would like to rent ...	Querría ... alquilar
a car/a bicycle/a boat	un coche/una bicicleta/un barco
petrol/gas station	gasolinera
petrol/gas / diesel	gasolina/diesel
breakdown/repair shop	avería/taller

FOOD & DRINK

Could you please book a table for tonight for four?	Resérvenos, por favor, una mesa para cuatro personas para hoy por la noche.
on the terrace/by the window	en la terraza/junto a la ventana
The menu, please	¡El menú, por favor!

Could I please have ...?	¿Podría traerme ... por favor?
bottle/carafe/glass	botella/jarra/vaso
knife/fork/spoon	cuchillo/tenedor/cuchara
salt/pepper/sugar	sal/pimienta/azúcar
vinegar/oil/milk/cream/lemon	vinagre/aceite/leche/limón
cold/too salty/not cooked	frío/demasiado salado/sin hacer
with/without ice/sparkling	con/sin hielo/gas
vegetarian/allergy	vegetariano/vegetariana/alergía
May I have the bill, please?	Querría pagar, por favor.
bill/receipt/tip	cuenta/recibo/propina

SHOPPING

pharmacy/chemist	farmacia/droguería
baker/market	panadería/mercado
butcher/fishmonger	carnicería/pescadería
shopping centre/department store	centro comercial/grandes almacenes
shop/supermarket/kiosk	tienda/supermercado/quiosco
100 grammes/1 kilo	cien gramos/un kilo
expensive/cheap/price/more/less	caro/barato/precio/más/menos
organically grown	de cultivo ecológico

ACCOMMODATION

I have booked a room	He reservado una habitación.
Do you have any ... left?	¿Tiene todavía ...?
single room/double room	habitación individual/habitación doble
breakfast/half board/	desayuno/media pensión/
full board (American plan)	pensión completa
at the front/seafront/garden view	hacia delante/hacia el mar/hacia el jardín
shower/sit-down bath	ducha/baño
balcony/terrace	balcón/terraza
key/room card	llave/tarjeta
luggage/suitcase/bag	equipaje/maleta/bolso
swimming pool/spa/sauna	piscina/spa/sauna
soap/toilet paper/nappy (diaper)	jabón/papel higiénico/pañal
cot/high chair/nappy changing	cuna/trona/cambiar los pañales
deposit	anticipo/caución

BANKS, MONEY & CREDIT CARDS

bank/ATM/	banco/cajero automático/
pin code	número secreto
cash/credit card	en efectivo/tarjeta de crédito
bill/coin/change	billete/moneda/cambio

HEALTH

doctor/dentist/paediatrician	médico/dentista/pediatra
hospital/emergency clinic	hospital/urgencias
fever/pain/inflamed/injured	fiebre/dolor/inflamado/herido
diarrhoea/nausea/sunburn	diarrea/náusea/quemadura de sol
plaster/bandage/ointment/cream	tirita/vendaje/pomada/crema
pain reliever/tablet/suppository	calmante/comprimido/supositorio

POST, TELECOMMUNICATIONS & MEDIA

stamp/letter/postcard	sello/carta/postal
I need a landline phone card/	Necesito una tarjeta telefónica/
I'm looking for a prepaid card for my mobile	Busco una tarjeta prepago para mi móvil
Where can I find internet access?	¿Dónde encuentro un acceso a internet?
dial/connection/engaged	marcar/conexión/ocupado
socket/adapter/charger	enchufe/adaptador/cargador
computer/battery/	ordenador/batería/
rechargeable battery	batería recargable
e mail address/at sign (@)	(dirección de) correo electrónico/arroba
internet address (URL)	dirección de internet
internet connection/wifi	conexión a internet/wifi
e-mail/file/print	archivo/imprimir

LEISURE, SPORTS & BEACH

beach/sunshade/lounger	playa/sombrilla/tumbona
low tide/high tide/current	marea baja/marea alta/corriente

NUMBERS

0	cero	14	catorce
1	un, uno, una	15	quince
2	dos	16	dieciséis
3	tres	17	diecisiete
4	cuatro	18	dieciocho
5	cinco	19	diecinueve
6	seis	20	veinte
7	siete	100	cien, ciento
8	ocho	200	doscientos, doscientas
9	nueve	1000	mil
10	diez	2000	dos mil
11	once	10 000	diez mil
12	doce	1/2	medio
13	trece	1/4	un cuarto

NOTES

FOR YOUR NEXT HOLIDAY ...

MARCO POLO TRAVEL GUIDES

MARCO POLO

With ROAD ATLAS & PULL-OUT MAP

LAKE GARDA

NT BALDU WITH MOUNTAIN BIKE
le Car in Malcesine takes bikes too

"KISSES" IN SALO
...baceti

Travel with
Insider
Tips

MARCO POLO

With STREET ATLAS & PULL-OUT MAP

NEW YORK

ADOWS, WILD FLOWERS AND SKYSCRAPERS
s chic: the High Line in Chelsea

TAIL ON CLOUD NINE
ftop bar at 230 Fifth Street

Travel with
Insider
Tips

MARCO POLO

With ROAD ATLAS & PULL-OUT MAP

FRENCH RIVIERA
NICE, CANNES & MONACO

SPECTACULAR GRAND CANYON DU VERDON
Breath-taking scenery that takes some beating

SNIFFING THE AIR
The perfume manufacturers of Grasse

Travel with
Insider
Tips

www.marco-polo.com

MARCO POLO

With ROAD ATLAS & PULL OUT MAP

ALLORCA

AN FLAIR IN THE MEDITERRANEAN
Mallorca's most beautiful beach

E, IN" CROWD MEET
onda in Deia

Travel with
Insider
Tips

MARCO POLO

With STREET ATLAS & PULL-OUT MAP

BERLIN

A STUNNING ISLAND JUST FOR ART
Showcasing treasures from around the world

STAY COOL AT NIGHT
scene sets the trend

Travel with
Insider
Tips

- PACKED WITH INSIDER TIPS
- BEST WALKS AND TOURS
- FULL-COLOUR PULL-OUT MAP
  AND STREET ATLAS

ROAD ATLAS

The green line ▬▬▬ indicates the Trips & Tours (p. 96–101)
The blue line ▬▬▬ indicates The perfect route (p. 30–31)

All tours are also marked on the pull-out map

Photo: Playa de las Teresitas

A

1

2 km
1.24 mi

B

C

2

ATLÁ

3

O C É A N O

4

Punta de Barranc

La

★★

**PUERTO
DE LA CRUZ**

Lomo Ro

Cuesta la Vi
la Orotava

Playa del An

★ **12**

Lago de Martíanez
N.S. de la Peña
de Francia

San Telmo
La Paz

Playa
Bollullo

El Rincón

5

Playa Jardín
Cast. de San Felipe

Punta
Piedra Gorda

Punta Brava

Playa de Gordejuela

Punta
El Guindastes

La Romántica
La Longuera

Loro
Parque

Las
Arenas

San Bartolomé

★ **5**

Jardín Botánico

El Guanche

TF5

★★

Bananera

P.C.

Orotava / P.C.

La Marzagan

San

La Oratava / La

La Dehi
Baja

La Matanza

San
Montijos

Valle de

El Camino
de Chasna
Los Camino

6

Playa de las Aguas

a de Marrero
ya de San
Agustín
Agustín

Las
Aguas

La
Rambla

Playa del Socorro

San Vicente

La Gorbonana

San Agustín

La Higuerita

San
Jerónimo

La
Orotava

Iglesia de N.S.
de la
Concepción

San Juan
de la Rambla

Icod el Alto

El Lance

Los Realejos

La Carrera

P.C.

La Montaneta La Candia
Tierra de Oro

San
Antonio

Cruz Santa

La
Perdoma

Palo Blanco

El Viñatico

Benijos

Las Llanadas

Los
Quevedos

La Vera

El Camino
de Chasna
Los Camino

(63)

San Isidro

Iglesia
de Santiago

La Puente

★ **9**

TF324

2.5 Lla

★ **15**

TF342

Tigaiga

Realejo
Alto

TF21

La Guancha

Las Rosas

Fuentes
del Bardo

La
Sombrerera

**L o s
R e a l e j o s**

★ **4**

(345)

TF326

896

Yopete

TF344

134

Cueva
de la Cazadora

128

29

Ba
Be

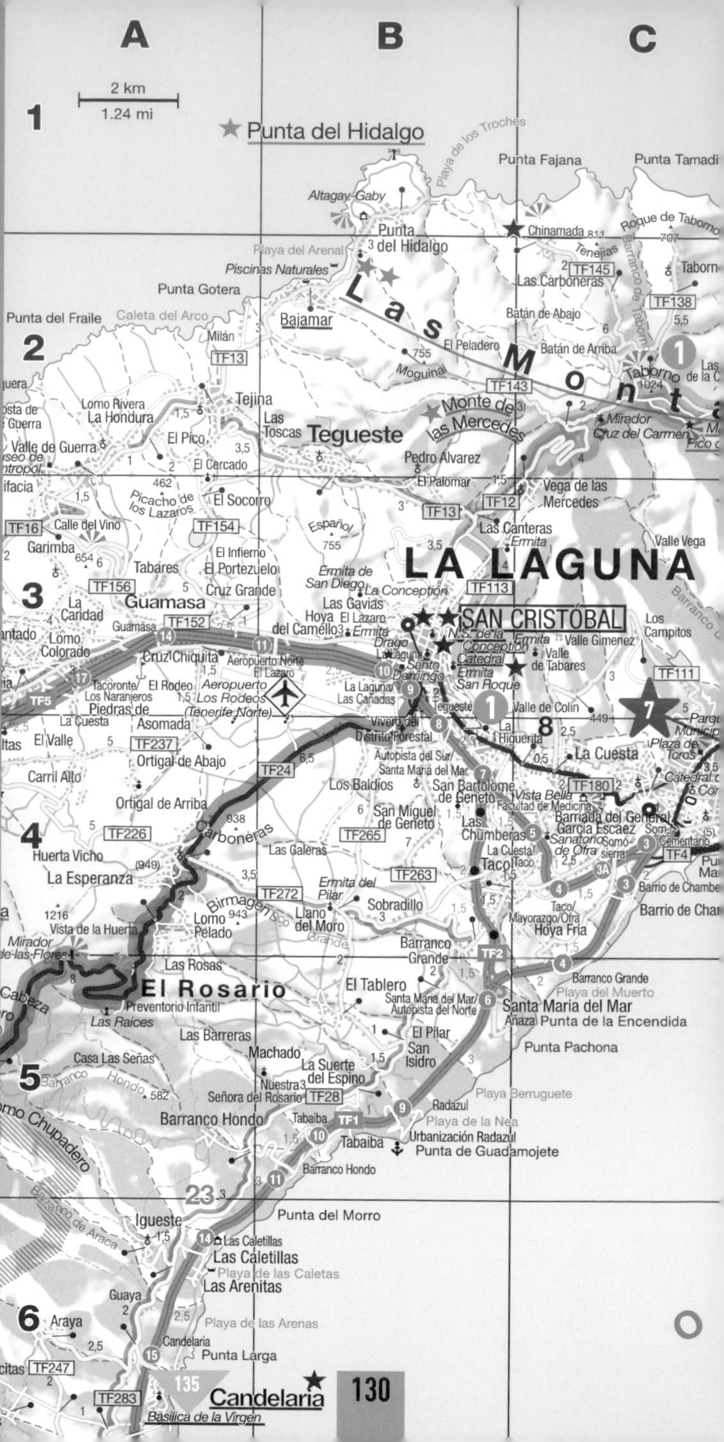
A
B
C
1
2
3
4
5
6
2 km
1.24 mi
Punta del Hidalgo
Playa de los Troches
Punta Fajana
Punta Tamadi
Altagay-Gaby
Chinamada
Roque de Taborno
Punta del Hidalgo
Playa del Arenal
Piscinas Naturales
Tenejías
Barranco de Taborno
Las Carboneras
TF145
Taborno
Punta Gotera
Las Montañas
TF138
Punta del Fraile
Caleta del Arco
Bajamar
Batán de Abajo
Milán
El Peladero
Batán de Arriba
TF13
Moguinal
TF143
Lomo Rivera
Tejina
Monte de las Mercedes
La Hondura
Las Toscas
Tegueste
Mirador Cruz del Carmen
Valle de Guerra
El Pico
Pedro Alvarez
El Cercado
El Palomar
Vega de las Mercedes
Picacho de los Lazaros
El Socorro
TF12
TF16
Calle del Vino
TF154
Español
Las Canteras
Ermita
Garimba
El Infierno
El Portezuelo
LA LAGUNA
Valle Vega
Tabares
Ermita de San Diego
TF156
Cruz Grande
La Concepción
TF113
La Caridad
Guamasa
Las Gavias
SAN CRISTÓBAL
Los Campitos
Hoya del Camello
El Lazaro
Ermita
Lomo Colorado
TF152
Drago
N.S. de la Concepción
Ermita
Valle Gimenez
Cruz Chiquita
Aeropuerto Norte
La Laguna
Catedral
Valle de Tabares
El Lazaro
Santo Domingo
Ermita San Roque
TF111
Tacoronte/ Los Naranjeros
El Rodeo
Aeropuerto Los Rodeos (Tenerife Norte)
La Laguna/ Las Cañadas
TF5
Piedras de Asomada
Tegueste
Valle de Colín
La Cuesta
Vivero del Distrito Forestal
La Higuerita
El Valle
TF237
La Cuesta
Plaza de Toros
Ortigal de Abajo
Autopista del Sur/ Santa María del Mar
TF24
TF180
Carril Alto
Los Baldíos
San Bartolomé de Geneto
Vista Bella
Facultad de Medicina
Ortigal de Arriba
San Miguel de Geneto
Barriada del General García Escaez
TF226
Carboneras
TF265
Las Chumberas
Sanatorio de Ofra
Somosierra
Cementario
Huerta Vicho
Las Galeras
La Cuesta/ Taco
TF4
La Esperanza
TF263
Taco
Ermita del Pilar
TF272
Barrio de Chambe
Birmagen Bco.
Sobradillo
Barrio de Cha
Lomo Pelado
Llano del Moro
Taco/ Mayorazgo/Ofra
Hoya Fria
Vista de la Huerta
Barranco Grande
Mirador de las Flores
TF2
Las Rosas
Barranco Grande
El Rosario
El Tablero
Playa del Muerto
Preventorio Infantil
Santa María del Mar/ Autopista del Norte
Santa María del Mar
Las Raices
Añaza
Punta de la Encendida
Las Barreras
El Pilar
Punta Pachona
Casa Las Señas
Machado
San Isidro
La Suerte del Espino
Barranco Hondo
Nuestra Señora del Rosario
TF28
Playa Berruguete
Radazul
Barranco Hondo
Tabaiba
TF1
Playa de la Nea
Lomo Chupadero
Tabaiba
Urbanización Radazul
Punta de Guadamojete
Barranco Hondo
23
Barranco de Araca
Punta del Morro
Igueste
Las Caletillas
Las Caletillas
Playa de las Caletas
Las Arenitas
Guaya
Playa de las Arenas
Araya
Candelaria
TF247
Punta Larga
TF283
135
Candelaria
Basílica de la Virgen

Roque de Fuera

Roque de Tierra

Punta de los Roquetes

Las Palmas

El Draguillo

Faro de Anaga
Roque Bermejo
Casas Blancas

Poyata

Playa de Benijo

Playa de
San Roque

Benijo

Chamorga

N.S.ª de la
Nieves

TF134

Almáciga

Taganana

Punta del Drago

Chinobre

Lomo
de las Bodegas

Barranco
de Añosma

B.ºo de la Iglesia

El Bailadero

TF123

910   10

Punta de Anaga

3,5

Azanos

Paso

1,5

F12   934

Barranco de las Huertas

Lomo Bermejo

Semáforo

Igueste   427

Punta de Antequera

Playa de Antequera

563

TF12

TF121

El Roquete

Roque Chiguel

Valle Brosque

695

Playa de las Gaviotas

9

El Roque

Punta de los Organos

318

8

Playa de las Teresitas ★

San Andrés

TF11

Dársena Pesquera

Boca del
Valle

rio-de-la-Alegría

Nautico

6

Ciencias Naturales ★

ANTA CRUZ

TENERIFE ★★

Santa Cruz de la Palma

Las Palmas de Gran Canaria

Agaete (Gran Canaria)

ATLÁNTICO

ANO

D   E   F

1

2

3

4

5

6

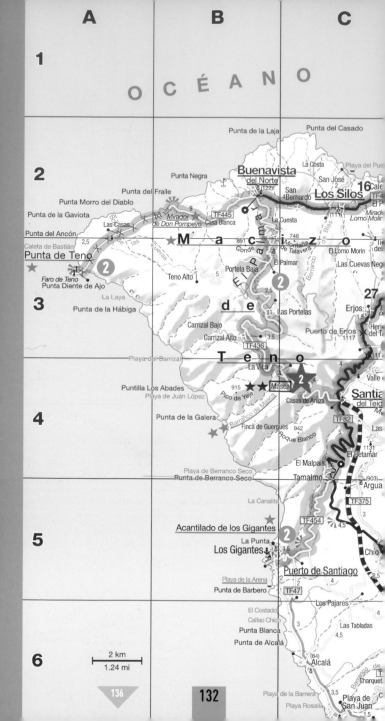

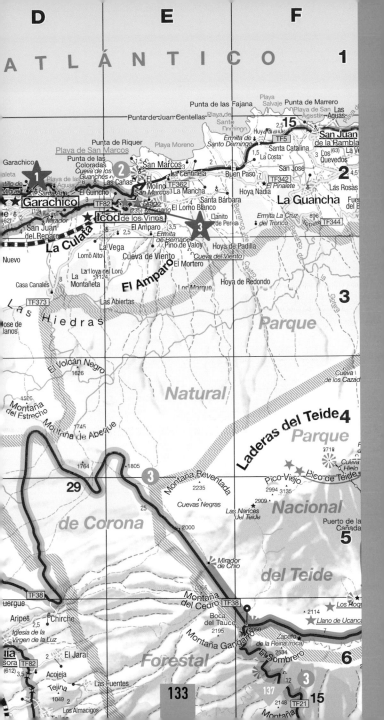

D   **E**   **F**

A T L Á N T I C O   **1**

Punta de las Fajana
Playa
Salvaje
Punta de Marrero
Playa de San
Agustín
Las
Aguas

Punta de Juan Centellas
Playa de
Santo
Domingo
Hoya Grande
2,5

15

Ermita de
Santo Domingo
TF5
**San Juan
de la Rambla**

Punta de Riquer
Playa Moreno
Santa Catalina
La Costa
Los
Quevedos
(63)

Playa de San Marcos
Punta de las
Coloradas
Cueva de los
Guanches
1,5
San Marcos
3
San José
896
Topete
TF342
El Pinalete
7
Las Rosas
2

Garachico
aleta
Santa Ana
Playa de las
Aguas
El Guincho
Las Cañas
El
Molino
TF362
San Marcos
(235)
Drago
Milenario
La Centinela
La Mancha
Buen Paso
Hoya Nadia
La Guancha
Fuer
del C

1

castillo de
Miguel
Garachico
TF82
Icod de los Vinos
El Lomo Blanco
Llanito
de Perea
Ermita La Cruz
del Tronco
TF344

2

e
(62)
Mirador
**San Juan
del Reparo**
El Amparo
2,5
Santa Bárbara

3

La Culata
La Vega
Ermita
de Bernabé
Pino de Valoy
Hoya de Padilla
Cueva del Viento

Nuevo
Lomo Alto
Cueva de Viento
El Mortero
Hoya de Redondo

Casa Canales
La llloya del Loró
1124
La
Montañeta
8
El Amparo
Los Marque

Parque

3

Las
H i e d r a s
Las Abiertas

ose de
lanos
TF373

Natural

El Volcán Negro
1626
Cueva
de los Cazad

Montaña
del Estrecho
1526

Laderas del Teide **4**

Montaña de Abeque
1745

Parque

1764
1805
3718

Cueva
Hielo

29
3
Montaña Reventada
2235
Pico Viejo
2994 3135
Pico de Teide

25
Cuevas Negras
2909
Las Narices
del Teide

Nacional

de Corona
2000
Puerto de la
Cañada

5

Mirador
de Chío

del Teide

uergue
TF38
2055
Montaña
del Cedro
TF38
2114
Los Roqu

Aripe
Chirche
2,5
Boca
del Tauce
2195
Llano de Ucanca

Iglesia de la
Virgen de la Luz
Montaña Gangaro
2050
Zapato
de la Reina (roca)
7

ía
sora
TF82
El Jaral
2534
El Sombrero

6

El Jaral
Acojeja
F o r e s t a l
7
12
3

Tejina
1049
Las Fuentes
133
137
2148
TF21
15

Los Almácigos
Montaña

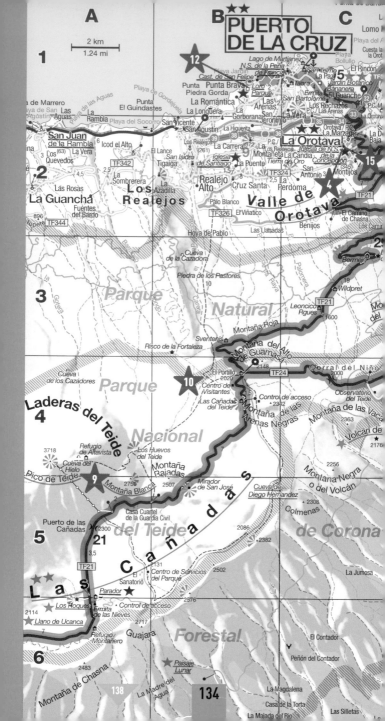

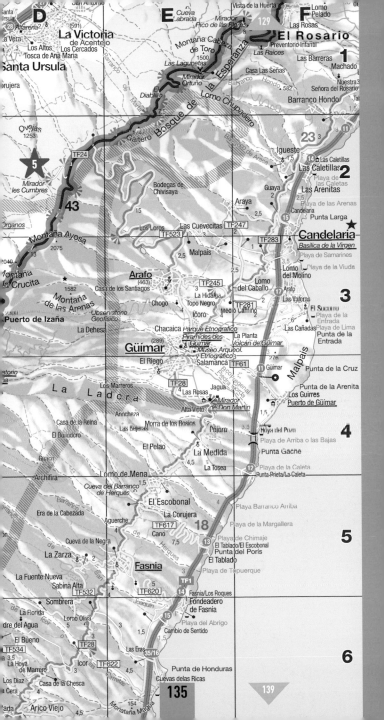

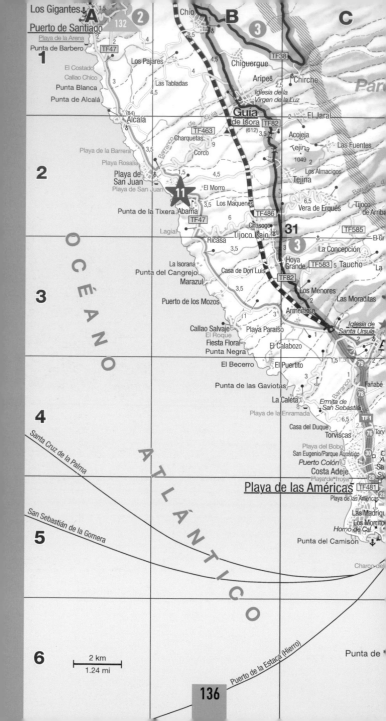

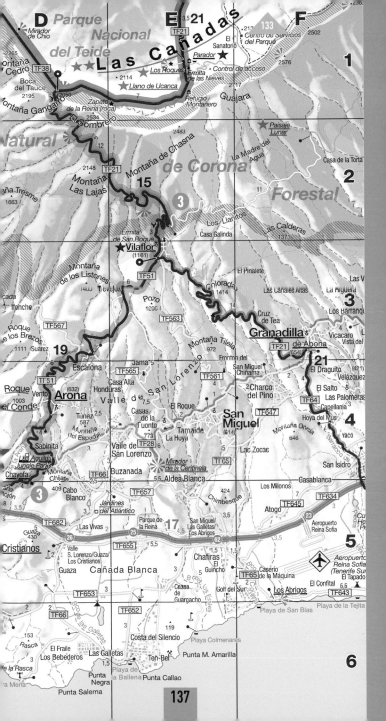

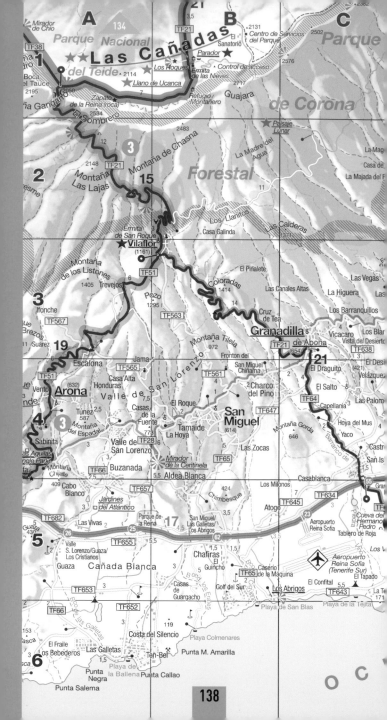

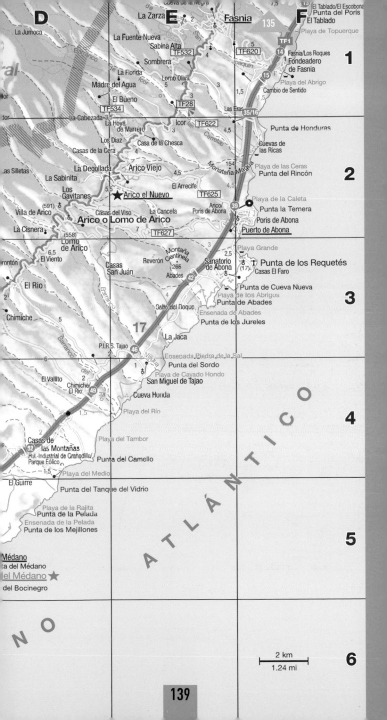

La Jumoca
La Zarza
Fasnia
El Tablado/El Escobano
Punta del Porís
El Tablado
Playa de Topuerque

La Fuente Nueva
Sabina Alta
TF532
Sombrera
La Florida
Madre del Agua
El Bueno
TF534
TF620
TF1
Fasnia/Los Roques
Fondeadero
de Fasnia

Lomo Oliva
TF28
Las Eras
35/16

1

Playa del Abrigo
Cambio de Sentido

La-Cabezada-3,5
La Hoya
de Marrero
Icor
TF622
Punta de Honduras

Los Díaz
Casas de la Cera
Casa de la Chesca
Cuevas de
las Ricas

La Degollada
Arico Viejo
Montaña Magua
154
Playa de las Ceras
Punta del Rincón

La Sabinita
Los
Gavitanes
El Arrecife
TF625
Playa de la Caleta
Punta la Ternera

las Silletas
★ Arico el Nuevo
Arico/
Porís de Abona
Poris de Abona

Villa de Arico
(591)
Casas del Viso
La Cancela
Puerto de Abona

La Cisnera
Arico o Lomo de Arico
TF627

2

Lomo
de Arico
(558)
Montaña
Centinela
Playa Grande

El Viento
6,5
Reverón
265
Sanatorio
de Abona
Punta de los Requetés
Casas El Faro

El Río
Casas
San Juán
Abades
42
Punta de Cueva Nueva
Punta de Abades

Chimiche
Salto del Noque
Playa de los Abrigos
Ensenada de Abades
Punta de los Jureles

3

17
La Jaca

P.I.R.S. Tajao
46
Ensenada Piedra de la Sal
Punta del Sordo

El Vallito
Chimiche/
El Río
49
San Miguel de Tajao
Playa de Cayado Hondo

Cueva Honda

Playa del Río

4

Casas de
las Montañas
92
Pol. Industrial de Granadilla/
Parque Eólico
Playa del Tambor
Punta del Camello

El Güirre
Playa del Medio
Punta del Tanque del Vidrio

Playa de la Rajita
Punta de la Pelada
Ensenada de la Pelada
Punta de los Mejillones

5

Médano
ta del Médano
el Médano ★
del Bocinegro

A T L Á N T I C O

6

2 km
1,24 mi

KEY TO ROAD ATLAS

Autobahn · Gebührenpflichtige Anschlussstelle · Gebührenstelle · Anschlussstelle mit Nummer · Rasthaus mit Übernachtung · Raststätte · Kleinraststätte · Tankstelle · Parkplatz mit und ohne WC		Motorway · Toll junction · Toll station · Junction with number · Motel · Restaurant · Snackbar · Filling-station · Parking place with and without WC
Autobahn in Bau und geplant mit Datum der Verkehrsübergabe		Motorway under construction and projected with completion date
Zweibahnige Straße (4-spurig)		Dual carriageway (4 lanes)
Fernverkehrsstraße · Straßennummern		Trunk road · Road numbers
Wichtige Hauptstraße		Important main road
Hauptstraße · Tunnel · Brücke		Main road · Tunnel · Bridge
Nebenstraßen		Minor roads
Fahrweg · Fußweg		Track · Footpath
Wanderweg (Auswahl)		Tourist footpath (selection)
Eisenbahn mit Fernverkehr		Main line railway
Zahnradbahn, Standseilbahn		Rack-railway, funicular
Kabinenschwebebahn · Sessellift		Aerial cableway · Chair-lift
Autofähre · Personenfähre		Car ferry · Passenger ferry
Schifffahrtslinie		Shipping route
Naturschutzgebiet · Sperrgebiet		Nature reserve · Prohibited area
Nationalpark · Naturpark · Wald		National park · natural park · Forest
Straße für Kfz. gesperrt		Road closed to motor vehicles
Straße mit Gebühr		Toll road
Straße mit Wintersperre		Road closed in winter
Straße für Wohnanhänger gesperrt bzw. nicht empfehlenswert		Road closed or not recommended for caravans
Touristenstraße · Pass		Tourist route · Pass
Schöner Ausblick · Rundblick · Landschaftlich bes. schöne Strecke		Scenic view · Panoramic view · Route with beautiful scenery
Heilbad · Schwimmbad		Spa · Swimming pool
Jugendherberge · Campingplatz		Youth hostel · Camping site
Golfplatz · Sprungschanze		Golf-course · Ski jump
Kirche im Ort, freistehend · Kapelle		Church · Chapel
Kloster · Klosterruine		Monastery · Monastery ruin
Synagoge · Moschee		Synagogue · Mosque
Schloss, Burg · Schloss-, Burgruine		Palace, castle · Ruin
Turm · Funk-, Fernsehturm		Tower · Radio-, TV-tower
Leuchtturm · Kraftwerk		Lighthouse · Power station
Wasserfall · Schleuse		Waterfall · Lock
Bauwerk · Marktplatz, Areal		Important building · Market place, area
Ausgrabungs- u. Ruinenstätte · Bergwerk		Arch. excavation, ruins · Mine
Dolmen · Menhir · Nuraghen		Dolmen · Menhir · Nuraghe
Hünen-, Hügelgrab · Soldatenfriedhof		Cairn · Military cemetery
Hotel, Gasthaus, Berghütte · Höhle		Hotel, inn, refuge · Cave

Kultur
Malerisches Ortsbild · Ortshöhe	**WIEN** (171)	Picturesque town · Elevation
Eine Reise wert	★★ **MILANO**	Worth a journey
Lohnt einen Umweg	★ TEMPLIN	Worth a detour
Sehenswert	_Andermatt_	Worth seeing

Landschaft / **Landscape**
Eine Reise wert	★★ Las Cañadas	Worth a journey
Lohnt einen Umweg	★ Texel	Worth a detour
Sehenswert	_Dikti_	Worth seeing

Ausflüge & Touren		**Excursions & tours**
Perfekte Route		**Perfect route**
MARCO POLO Highlight	⭐**1**	**MARCO POLO Highlight**

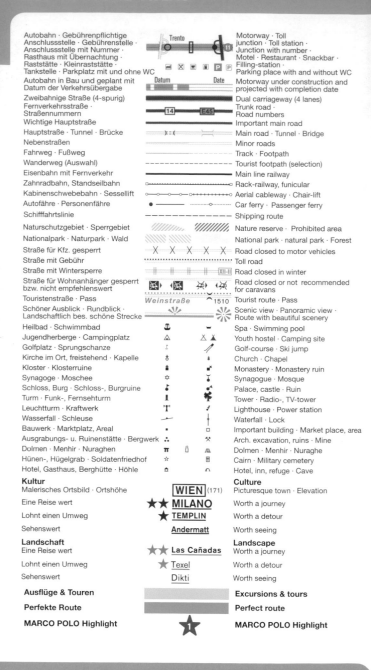

INDEX

This index lists all sights, museums and destinations plus the main squares and streets, the key terms and people featured in this guide. Numbers in bold indicate a main entry

WRITE TO US

e-mail: info@marcopologuides.co.uk

Did you have a great holiday?
Is there something on your mind?
Whatever it is, let us know!
Whether you want to praise, alert us to errors or give us a personal tip – MARCO POLO would be pleased to hear from you.
We do everything we can to provide the very latest information for your trip.

Nevertheless, despite all of our authors' thorough research, errors can creep in. MARCO POLO does not accept any liability for this. Please contact us by e-mail or post.

MARCO POLO Travel Publishing Ltd
Pinewood, Chineham Business Park
Crockford Lane, Chineham
Basingstoke, Hampshire RG24 8AL
United Kingdom

PICTURE CREDITS
Cover photograph: Mount Teide and flowers (alamy/PCL: picturescolourlibrary)
Photos: O. Baumli (110/111); DuMont Bildarchiv. Schwarzbach/Schroder (28/29, 37, 110); © fotolia.com: Tony Bartlett (16 centre), Rohit Seth (16 bottom); R. Freyer (2 centre, 2 bottom, 12, 18/19, 24/25, 26 left, 32/33, 34/35, 40/41, 48/49, 52/53, 54, 58/59, 61, 62, 67, 87, 98, 99); I. Gawin (1 bottom, 8, 30 right, 74) ; Getty Images/Photodisc: C Squared Studios (1 top), R. Hackenberg (flap right, 57); Huber: Mirau (3 top, 68/69), Schmid (1 top, 10/11, 47); ITER - Instituto Tecnológico y de Energías Renovables, S.A. (16 top, 17 top); Laif. Eid (50), hemis.fr (30 left), Sasse (91, 101, 114 top), Tophoven (80, 84); Laif/hemis.fr: Frilet (92/93); Look: age fotostock (105, 114 bottom.); mauritius images: AGE (26 right), Alamy (2 top, 2 centre top , 3 bottom, 5, 6, 7, 9, 14/15, 22, 45, 77, 78/79, 82, 88, 115), Cubolmages (64/65), Flüeler (42); mauritius images/imagebroker: Kreder (3 centre, 72/73), Sarti (4); D. Renckhoff (28, 102/103, 104, 111); W. Storto (71); Tenerife Outdoor: Victor Teni (17 bottom); White Star: Gumm (flap left, 27), 29, 46, 89, 108, 126/127); T. P. Widmann (94, 96/97, 106/107); E. Wrba (20)

1st Edition 2013
Worldwide Distribution: Marco Polo Travel Publishing Ltd, Pinewood, Chineham Business Park, Crockford Lane, Basingstoke, Hampshire RG24 8AL, United Kingdom. Email: sales@marcopolouk.com
© MAIRDUMONT GmbH & Co. KG, Ostfildern
Chief editors: Michaela Lienemann (concept, managing editor), Marion Zorn (concept, text editor)
Author: Sven Weniger, Co-author: Izabela Gawin; Editor: Arnd M. Schuppius
Programme supervision: Ann-Katrin Kutzner, Nikolai Michaelis, Silwen Randebrock
Picture editor: Gabriele Forst
What's hot: wunder media, Munich;
Cartography road atlas: © MAIRDUMONT, Ostfildern; Cartography pull-out map: © MAIRDUMONT, Ostfildern
Design: milchhof : atelier, Berlin; Front cover, pull-out map cover, page 1: factor product munich
Translated from German by Paul Fletcher, Suffolk; editor of the English edition: Tony Halliday, Oxford
Prepress: BW-Medien GmbH, Leonberg
Phrase book in cooperation with Ernst Klett Sprachen GmbH, Stuttgart, Editorial by Pons Wörterbücher

DOS & DON'TS

A few things to bear in mind on Tenerife

DON'T BE TAKEN IN BY THE DREAM HOLIDAY FRAUDSTERS

You will probably be approached by aggressive touts trying to sell dubious holiday packages. Formerly known as timesharing, holiday homes are now marketed as 'timeshare clubs', 'holiday packs' or 'holiday clubs', In fact, that dream apartment on a sun-drenched island will almost certainly turn out to be a nightmare. Expect to have to make a down payment of thousands of euros. Buyer beware.

DON'T LEAVE VALUABLES IN YOUR CAR

Hire cars are often broken into, and bags and wallets stolen from the beach or hotel room. So don't leave anything of value visible in your car or in the boot. Similarly make sure anything of value is locked away in your room or apartment safe. If no safe is available, then leave any valuables at reception.

DON'T GET FLEECED IN A RESTAURANT

In Spain bread is part of every meal. It used to be offered free of charge. Now it is served as a matter of course … but then a charge made after the meal. If you are justifiably dissatisfied in a restaurant, then ask for a hojas de reclamación (complaint form), so that you can put your criticism in writing. Every restaurant must provide these forms; the complaints system is overseen by the Spanish authorities.

DON'T HAVE UNPROTECTED SEX

Surveys taken of tourists under the age of 26 have shown that 50 percent of them had sex with a new partner. Doctors say that there is an increasing risk of contracting HIV or other sexually-transmitted diseases. So act responsibly and make sure you protect yourself and others!

DON'T JOIN A 'FREE' COACH TOUR

Leaflets distributed on the streets repeatedly lure unsuspecting tourists into joining free island tours with tempting offers of free coffee and cakes. Many people accept these trips in good faith, but they are then subjected to a persuasive sales pitch for overpriced, poor quality goods. Stay well away from these excursions.

DON'T BUY FAKE BRANDED GOODS

Only buy watches, electronic goods and branded fashion items in department stores and reputable shops. Bargains at bazaars and flea markets nearly always turn out to be fakes. Customs can confiscate such goods and impose a fine.

DON'T USE THE HOTEL INTERNET NETWORK

Many hotels make internet access available for guests. But the charges can often be very high. Internet access should be free these days.